Rooted

Your Sure Hope in the Storms of Life

Mike Novotny

Published by Straight Talk Books
P.O. Box 301, Milwaukee, WI 53201
800.661.3311 • timeofgrace.org

Copyright © 2019 Time of Grace Ministry

All rights reserved. This publication may not be copied, photocopied, reproduced, translated, or converted to any electronic or machine-readable form in whole or in part, except for brief quotations, without prior written approval from Time of Grace Ministry.

Scripture is taken from THE HOLY BIBLE, NEW INTERNATIONAL VERSION®, NIV®. Copyright © 1973, 1978, 1984, 2011 by Biblica, Inc.® Used by permission. All rights reserved worldwide.

Printed in the United States of America
ISBN: 978-1-949488-20-3

TIME OF GRACE and IT ALL STARTS NOW are registered marks of Time of Grace Ministry.

Contents

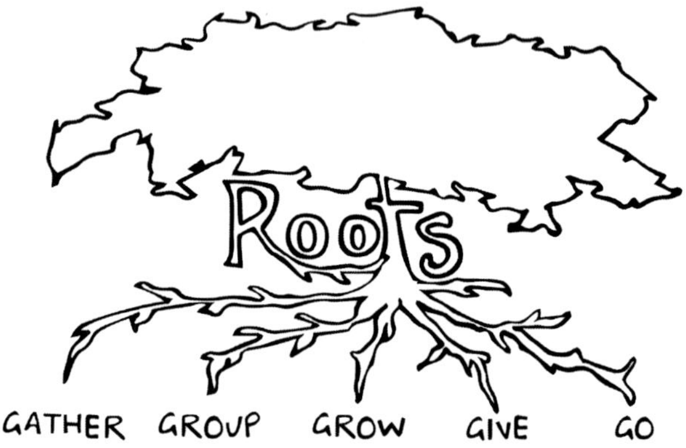
Roots
GATHER GROUP GROW GIVE GO

Introduction

Have you ever noticed that some of the best things in life can't be produced in a second, but they have to be grown? When it comes to good character, when it comes to good kids, when it comes to a strong body, it's so much more than saying a quick prayer and waking up the next morning. These require a step-by-step process that leads to something really good.

Think about pineapple, for example. I love pineapple. I'm not talking pineapple in a can with those pale, yellow chunks floating in juice. I'm talking about fresh pineapple. I'm talking about cored and sliced from the grocery store. I'm talking about a fresh pineapple ring on the grill that you put on a burger with bacon and mayo. I'm talking about steak tacos with pineapple salsa. I'm thinking about one of my favorite restaurants in Madison, Wisconsin, that serves all you can eat sliced pineapple covered in cinnamon for dessert. Last time I was there, I asked the waiter, "How many of these can you order until you think I'm 'that guy'?" Then I totally ignored the answer that he gave me. Do you enjoy fresh pineapple? If you don't, I'm about to question your salvation. It's one of God's greatest gifts to humanity.

I watched a four-minute YouTube video the other day, and here's what I learned: Pineapple doesn't just pop out of the ground. It's a process. According to the video I watched from Dole—you know, the kings of pineapple growing—it takes about 13 to 16 months from the first planting of the seed and the root until there's a fresh pineapple to enjoy.

I'm writing about this, not to persuade you in the gospel of fresh pineapple, but I'm thinking about your character and your faith and your relationship with God right now. If you've started following Jesus for any amount of time, you know that a strong faith isn't something you pray for and there it is. It's a patient process, but it's a predictable one. If you plant the right seeds and have the right roots, God will bring back some incredible fruit.

Read this great passage from the Bible's New Testament in Galatians 5:22,23. The apostle Paul says this: **"The fruit of the Spirit is love, joy, peace, forbearance** [patience], **kindness, goodness, faithfulness, gentleness and self-control."** I want you to look at that passage and think about what your life is like when you have lots of that fruit. Then think about what life is like when you don't. Think about if your church or your family or your relationship or your school or your workplace has tons of that compared to when it has none of that. And you start to

If you plant the right seeds and have the right roots, God will bring back some incredible fruit.

realize why this fruit is so good.

Think about the fruit of love. If you go to a church and there's no love, if you go and find your seat and no one cares and there's no compassion or encouragement, I bet you won't enjoy it. But if you walk in and the place is bursting with love, people who want to do life together, who want to encourage you, who want to see you grow in your faith, how good is that church?

Growing up in a home where your mom and dad have lots of this fruit is another example. When Dad is faithful to Mom and Mom is kind to Dad. When Dad's love of Jesus brings joy into the home and Mom's trust in the power of her heavenly Father brings peace in the midst of crazy circumstances. If your parents have fruit, how blessed are you?

Think about the fruit of peace. You have that fruit when you don't have to fall asleep at the end of the day wondering if you're good enough for God to like you, but you know that because of what Jesus did it's all good. God doesn't put up with you or let you sneak in the back door of heaven. He loves you, he likes you, he delights in you, he rejoices over you, and if you don't have to live with any of the guilt or shame or questions, then the fruit of peace is one of the best things that you can imagine. I could go on . . . When you have the fruit of self-control versus sin. When you start dating someone and she's filled with patience and gentleness and goodness. Fruit makes life really, really good.

But here's the thing about that fruit: It's fruit. The apostle Paul picked that word intentionally. He didn't say the "miracle of the Spirit," as if you could pray and there it would be in the morning. He didn't say the "result of prayer," as if you could say, "in Jesus' name" and open your eyes and there it would be. He said, "The fruit." Because just like a pineapple needs time to grow, the Holy Spirit needs time to work in your heart until he produces an

The Holy Spirit needs time to work in your heart.

abundance of this kind of fruit. That's why if you read or listen to me for more than one or two weeks, you'll hear me talk about good fruit and about good roots. If you were to walk into my church today, you might notice a giant tree with big fruit and massive roots in the lobby. You might see the same tree on the front of your program. If you saw our emails, checked out our Facebook or Instagram, you'd see that we don't go more than 24 hours at our church without talking about roots and fruit. We often talk about the five roots that produce that incredible fruit. It's something we call "Gather, Group, Grow, Give, and Go." By *Gather*, we mean we gather together in church week after week. By *Group*, we mean we do life together with other Christians. By *Grow*, we mean we're trying to get into the Bible every day at home. By *Give*, we're giving generously like Jesus, our time and our talents. And by *Go*, we mean we're on a mission to tell people who don't have roots so they can enjoy the fruits of the Spirit too.

As you picture that great tree with its roots, I want you to think about your roots. How are they doing? If you had to rank those five things from your strongest root to a root that's kind of dinky to maybe a root that doesn't quite exist just yet, what would be your best and what would be your worst? I want you to think about that because I just read a 40-year-old article by a former professor of forestry from the University of North Carolina State. It was called "Tree Roots: Facts and Fallacies." Sounds pretty interesting, doesn't it? It was! The professor's name was Thomas Perry, and there was one quote from that study that jumped off the page and made me think of faith. Here's what Dr. Perry said, "If a large portion of the root system is destroyed, a corresponding portion of the leaves and branches will die." You get that, right? He's saying that if you cut a root off the bottom of a tree, the whole tree doesn't die, just the corresponding portion of its branches. In other words, if a tree has fewer roots, it will produce less fruit. On the contrary, if a tree has all of its roots, it will produce more fruit. Do you see what I'm getting at? When I mention Gather and Group and Grow and Give and Go, I'm not saying that if you don't give generously or you don't take time to read the Bible on a Tuesday night or sign up for a group, your faith will die and you won't end up with God in heaven. I am saying, though, that you will miss out on some of the best things that God wants to give—more fruit, more love, more joy, and more peace. So, if your heart is anything like mine and you want more joy and you want your marriage to have more love and you want to have more peace and trust in your heavenly Father, then there's a simple answer: Plant roots.

That's what I want to help you do in the next few chapters of this book. The official mission statement of my church is this: That we exist to help people. That's important. I exist as a pastor to help people plant Jesus' roots that produce the Spirit's fruit. So for the next few chapters, I want to not only write about what the roots are but why they are so good, why they are worth your time and energy and effort and planning. Because it might not happen today or tomorrow—like a good pineapple, it might take a year, maybe a little more—but in time, God will keep his promises and your roots will produce incredible fruit.

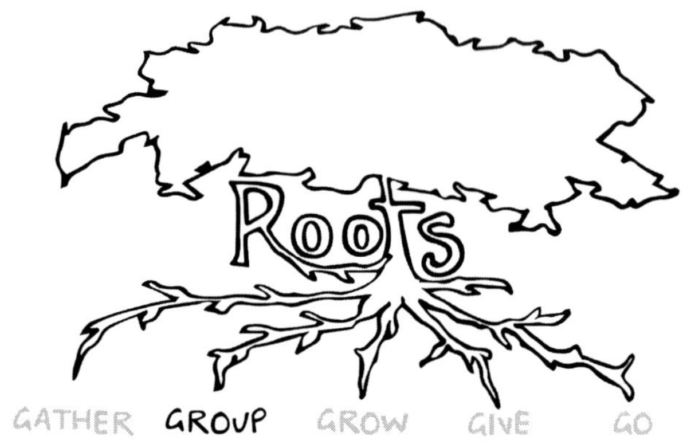
Roots
GATHER GROUP GROW GIVE GO

Get a Group

This is a little out of order from the tree mentioned in the Introduction, but let's start with the Group root. A group might be an official "life group" that's offered at a church, or it might be those small groups of Christians whom you do life with and carry out the "one another" passages of the Bible. So here's the purpose of this first chapter. If you want fruit, then God's encouragement to you is to get a group. Get connected to people who love Jesus, who love you, and fruit will come.

There are many passages in the Bible that I could use to make that point, but I want to focus on a single passage—one verse, that's all we're going to cover—Acts 2:42: **"They devoted themselves to the apostles' teaching and to fellowship,**

to the breaking of bread and to prayer." That passage is actually so famous in the Scriptures that there are some churches I've heard of in the U.S. that are named 242 Church, because they want the entire culture of their church to be based on that single passage.

Let's go back about two thousand years to when that passage was written. Jesus came as the Son of God, died on a cross for our sins, rose from the dead, stayed and preached and proved that he was risen from the dead for about 40 days, and then he returned to heaven. I want to take you to about a week after Jesus returned to heaven, ten days after his ascension. This is a day when the apostle Peter preached a powerful message, and the Holy Spirit went wild. He changed three thousand people's hearts on a single day. He added three thousand members to the holy Christian church. They were baptized, they became followers of Jesus, and they looked at each other and they said, "Well, now what?" And Acts 2:42 says exactly what the *what* was.

I want to show you four keys to a good group. The followers of Jesus whom I just mentioned devoted themselves to four specific things. By devoted, I mean they committed themselves to them. They said no to about one thousand things so they could say yes to these four things. They got into these habits, and they protected these habits so they could hang on until God produced the right amount of fruit in them. So that's what we're going to cover, the four keys to a good group.

The early church devoted themselves to the apostles' teaching.

Here's how Acts 2:42 begins: **"They,"** the early Christians, **"devoted themselves to the apostles' teaching."** That's the first thing the early church devoted themselves to—the apostles' teaching. The apostles, if you're kind of new to the Bible, were the 12 people whom Jesus handpicked to be his inner circle. What was their teaching? We don't have to guess what it was because the first 41 verses of Acts chapter 2 tell us. When the apostle Peter stood up, what he taught was Jesus—who Jesus was, what Jesus did, the cross of Jesus, the empty tomb of Jesus. He taught people to repent, to turn away from their sins, and to turn to Jesus for redemption and real life. They were devoted to the Bible and the Jesus who is the center of it.

The best groups of Christians do the same thing. They devote themselves, they are committed to, they get in the habit of holding to the teachings of the Bible. This might sound way too obvious, but can I tell you it's not quite that simple? I've been officially involved in small groups or life groups where 10 to 12 Christians get together in a room and try to do life together. I've been doing that for about ten years, and do you know what I've learned about most people? That in general, most people like to squirrel! They chase tangents all the time, and I do it too. In the course of a conversation, there are so many thoughts that pop into our heads. If we're not devoted or committed to the actual topic, the actual Scripture, we'll talk about everything except the Bible and the Jesus who's at the center of it. You might think I'm exaggerating, but sometimes I try to count the tangents. I've gotten to double-digit tangents in conversations and then wondered how these conversations got to where they did.

But that's how the human brain works, right? The conversation starts. "Hey, what'd you think about the message?" And the first person says, "Well, I don't know. I liked the parts about Jesus being like a shepherd or like a guy who sows seeds." And the second person says, "Oh yeah! That kind of reminds me; I grew up on a farm." And the third person says, "Hey, my cousin's actually a farmer. His name is Rob." Next person says, "Oh, I have a friend named Rob. He loves bacon." And the next person says, "Speaking of bacon, I love Kevin Bacon." And then someone pulls out her phone and starts the *Footloose* soundtrack. . . . Okay, I've kind of exaggerated, but not by much. We chase squirrels and tangents, and a whole hour can go by. We miss the message and the Jesus at the center of it. And so, the best groups have to be devoted. We can go on tangents, and we can have fun—I'm not saying we can't—but we have to actually commit our minds to hold on and get in the habit of wrestling with the Bible and not just sharing our own thoughts and opinions.

So if you have a Bible group, I really want you to be committed because groups are the perfect places to learn about Jesus. I love church, but church isn't really the environment to raise your hand and interrupt me to answer a question. I love it when people read the Bible and grow at home. I don't know about you, though, but often when I read the Bible, there's stuff that confuses me. But if God puts ten Christians in a room, how many years of Christian ex-

Be committed because groups are the perfect places to learn about Jesus.

perience has he gathered together? Even if some people are brand-new to the faith or not Christians at all, in a group of ten you might have 50- or 70- or 100-plus years of Christian knowledge. Some people might still be wet from their baptisms, but there are other people who have been following Jesus for decades. They've heard hundreds of sermons and read the Bible cover to cover, and they can help understand this beautiful but sometimes challenging book.

You might not even know what a Habakkuk is, but there's probably someone in your group who knows that Habakkuk was the prophet who the apostle Paul quoted in Romans chapter 1. And then five hundred years ago when the reformer Martin Luther read the quote in Romans, it helped him understand that we become right with God by faith because Habakkuk said the righteous person will live by faith. When a group is devoted to the apostles' teaching, you can feel comfortable saying, "You know, guys, I have no clue what that means. Can you help?" And if you're devoted to the apostles' teaching, you will teach one another, encourage one another, and grow together in incredible faith.

Do you know why especially I want you to be committed to that? Because some people are scared of groups. I've had conversations with people that go like this: "Pastor, I could never tell the church about that." There's some struggle, there's some embarrassing part of the past, and there's this fear of being real with other Christians. But think about this—if a group is devoted to the apostles' teaching and the teaching was essentially that Jesus has forgiven everything, then a group would be the safest place to share anything. In that group of people there aren't going to be a bunch of opinions and thoughts, but people will be devoted to how Jesus responded to sin, to abuse, to struggle, to addiction, to prostitution, to adultery, to anything. When you're committed to staying in the text, you can remind people, "You know that Jesus died for stuff like that too, don't you?" "You know that God still delights in you because you believe in Jesus, don't you?" "You know that we're not going to take a step back because somehow you're a worse sinner than us." Group is not a competition of who's the better Christian and who's more holy in the room. We all come with sin of our own, and Jesus was put on a cross for the forgiveness of sins. If we remember that, then group is the safest place on the planet. And group is where you can get a glimpse of the face of God who, when you confess to him, does not wrinkle up his nose in disgust but gushes with love and grace and mercy. And so, I don't just want you to join a group. I want that group to be committed to the Bible because the Jesus who's at the center of the Bible is the best thing in all of creation.

Jesus was put on a cross for the forgiveness of sins.

That brings us to the second thing the early church was devoted to. Back in Acts 2:42 it says, **"They devoted themselves to the apostles' teaching and to fellowship."**

They were also devoted to fellowship. *Fellowship* is just a fancy Bible word that means "mutual concern." So if you think that group is just about in-depth, intellectual Bible study, you've got it wrong. It's just as much about people as it is about passages. It's about people who have an actual love and concern that they would give up their own wealth, their own time, their own energy to show love to actual people whom God loves. If that sounds awesome, it is. What makes groups so good are the people, the encouragement, the faith, the knowledge, the prayers, the forgiveness.

Can I be real with you too though? The hardest thing about group is the people! Because people are really, really great on paper but in practice, they're people. I sometimes think—I know this is a little cheesy; my wife doesn't like this one—group is like a box of chocolates. You never know who you're going to get. Have you ever heard comedian Jim Gaffigan? He talks about Valentine's Day chocolates as gamble chocolates. You don't know what's inside each one, and when you show up to group, you don't know who's going to be inside that house. There might be people like you, and there might be some who aren't like you at all. Some might be wired the way you solve problems and think, and some might be on the opposite end of the spectrum. So fellowship, actual group, becomes a battleground for love. The fruit of the Spirit is patience and self-control and kindness and gentleness, and you will never know if you actually have those things if you only go to church. I could be the most annoying person on planet Earth, and you could shake my hand and find a seat on the other side of church. We'd be fine. But if you have to be with me week after week in the same room—now let's talk about love and commitment and patience and kindness and self-control.

In fact, I think that's why the Bible is as long as it is. Do you know why there are so many pages that finish out the New Testament? Why there's a Romans and Corinthians and another Corinthians and Galatians and Ephesians and Philippians and Colossians? It's because the early Christian church was filled with people. People weren't always perfect. Sometimes they believed weird things. Sometimes they had really bad behavior, and the apostle Paul had to write to them to encourage them because their churches were just like our groups; they had people.

When we actually love people—as the passage says, when we are "devoted" to people—when I'm not just going to sign up and show up when it's convenient and nice and easy for me but I believe that God has put me and put you in that room to learn to love people and to really grasp the heart of God, that's a great group. When you can find a group of people who actually care about one another's faith, that's a good group.

When we actually love people—that's a great group.

I was so proud of my congregation a couple months ago. There was this guy in our fellowship who was going through a really tough time in life. He needed a lot of encouragement. And I was going to help him, but I knew he needed more than just me, so I reached out to about a dozen people from my church and asked in an email, "Hey, would you be willing to write a letter to this brother in the faith to encourage him?" I was hoping that two or three or four people would commit themselves to encouraging this brother. Do you know what happened? Within an hour, I got a reply in my inbox: "I'd love to help, Pastor." And then another reply in my inbox: "Count us in, Pastor." And then a third and then a fourth and then a fifth reply, "We'll write every single week, Pastor." I saw the devotion to fellowship, and I talked to this guy and I realized how much it meant. He experienced something great because the people at my church are not just devoted to coming and hearing a message week after week, singing four songs, and going home. They are devoted to fellowship. That's my encouragement to you. If you take that step and you sign up for a group and God brings all kinds of people like you together, see that as your mission. A chance to grow, to bring joy, to give love, to produce fruit.

Next in Acts 2:42: **"They devoted themselves to the apostles' teaching and to fellowship, to the breaking of bread."** They were devoted to breaking bread. Now for about two thousand years, Christians have debated what that phrase means. In the Bible, sometimes breaking bread means sharing a meal together. And other times, breaking bread refers to what we call the Lord's Supper because Jesus broke bread and gave it to his disciples. There's power when you and I are devoted and committed to sharing meals together.

I just read a study that was published by the U.S. Loneliness Index. They did this massive study of Americans, and they tried to find out who are the loneliest people in America. Do you know what they found? You might think people in their 70s or 80s, many of which have buried their spouses, parents, and friends. But no. The loneliest group of Americans are between the ages of 18 and 22, which is interesting to me. If you're 18 to 22, what some people call Generation Z, you grew up as a digital native. You can't remember a time when the internet didn't exist. You grew up with devices and smartphones and tablets. You are connected every day and perhaps to more people than your great-grandparents would have shaken hands with in their entire lives. So how is it possible that you can be that connected, have that many likes, that many comments, and still feel lonelier than your grandparents?

I'm sure the answer to that question is pretty complicated and nuanced, but I wonder if part of it is this: The average 18- to 22-year-old doesn't break bread. They say that family dinners, people actually looking each other in the eye over a table and good food, are decreasing precipitously and our mental health is going with it. But what happens when we share a meal? When our communication is not carefully crafted and highlighted and deleted and rephrased, but we communicate with each other through what we say and through the expressions on our faces? What happens when we go out to dinner and put our phones facedown? It will be easier to tell when something is bothering the other person. When he or she is quiet and frustrated or when you can sense that I'm confused or have a question. When we can read each other and dig in and communication is not shallow because when we're face-to-face it's hard not to go deep. What happens when we're committed to breaking bread is that we grow. There's often kindness and goodness and faithfulness and love. The joy of the gospel and the peace of Jesus are shared when we share a meal.

I know how powerful that is because I've seen it in my church members. About a month ago, one of my friends who lives in Milwaukee visited our church. He's a really tall guy named Matt. After the service, we talked. In fact, we were talking a lot about group that day and he said, "You know what, Pastor? Being at your church gives me group envy." That's how he put it. He said, "I really wish I lived closer. I really wish I could sign up for a group." But afterward, he said something even more impactful. He said, "As I was leaving church, there was a noticeable buzz in the lobby." I know what he meant. I've preached at dozens of churches over the years, and I'm used to having a sore hand, you know, as the pastor stands at the exit and shakes hand after hand after hand as people bolt for their cars. But do you know what happens at my church? I'm shocked by how few people leave after a packed church service. There's a buzz in the lobby because the members are breaking bread or cookies or coffee or whatever they're sharing. And I know the church has a lot of strengths, and it has some significant weaknesses, but I think one of the secret sauces of my church is that from its inception, we never meant to just check this little box called church. We always wanted it to be real and relational. We wanted to have a relationship that went beyond Sunday. We actually wanted to do life together.

So that's why I want to encourage you with a group. I know sometimes you've got to leave church or a Bible group right away because sometimes life is busy. But if at all possible, can I encourage you to do this one thing? Stay for food. Sometimes it's not in the living room during the official group time; it's in the kitchen, where that big group of 12 will break off into conversations of 2 and 3. It's the place where real questions and digging deeper and real encouragement and the real grace of Jesus and real prayers and real forgiveness are given because we can do life together. The secret sauce of the early church is that they didn't just show up one day a week. They were devoted to teaching fellowship and to the breaking of bread.

And now for the final point in Acts 2:42: **"They devoted themselves to the apostles' teaching and to fellowship, to the breaking of bread and to prayer."** That was their final devotion; they were devoted to prayer. Can I be really honest with you? The Bible says my job description is to be really good at the Bible and prayer, and I'm bad at prayer. I'm not just trying to be humble. I'm good at the Word, I love reading the Bible at home, but I'm bad at prayer. I've tried to fix it. I've tried prayer apps. I've tried journaling. I've tried accountability. I've tried repeating events in my calendar. I've tried push notifications on my phone. I recently had to report to our lead pastor and tell him how many blocks of time I had prayed over the past two months for our church. Not random shotgun prayers, but when did I sit down and pray for my members? After two months, do you know how much time I had spent? Fifteen minutes. Yeah. But I'm not going to give up on prayer. I'm going to re-devote myself to praying for my members, and here's why: Because the devil fears people who persist in prayer. The devil knows that for those who keep knocking, the door will be opened. Those who keep seeking will find

The devil fears people who persist in prayer.

what they're looking for. Those who keep reaching out to Jesus will find him in the arms of faith. The early church devoted themselves to praying for each other, and when we do, good things happen.

I've seen it in group. I've been to plenty of Bible studies, and I love every kind of prayer; thank God for that. But sometimes prayer is shallow and generic and minds wander because it's nothing that we care about. In group, when people know each other, they can pray for a person's specific temptation or struggle. They can pray for a person by name and by situation, and God does really good things. My group shares cell numbers, and we pray for each other—not just week after week but day after day. I can put out a prayer request and say, "Hey, this Friday I'm going to face this, and I know it's going to be tempting. Would you pray for me?" Man, God does really, really good stuff. When we pray not just about safe travels and Grandma's cancer, but we pray about holiness and forgiveness and to escape shame and guilt, good stuff happens. When we pray the gospel over each other that we would believe everything that Jesus did, incredible things happen. When we don't see prayer just as a starter pistol to group or the official technicality that ends a church service but a privilege and a power source, great things happen. We devote ourselves to prayer. We commit ourselves to it. The past might stink, but we're not going to give up on the future because our Father in heaven loves to answer prayers in Jesus' name.

That's what the early church did, and it changed the world. You could threaten Christians, you could persecute them, and you could throw them to the lions. You could exclude them and mock them socially, but they were devoted to these things, and it changed the world. I hope it changes you too. If you'd read the last few verses of Acts chapter 2, you'd find out the fruit that came from that Group root.

Here's one last passage in Acts chapter 2. It says, **"They broke bread in their homes and ate together with glad and sin-**

cere hearts" (verse 46). There was gladness and happiness. There was joy, and there was peace. There was really good fruit because they planted really good roots.

I pray that you do the same thing. Maybe you've never had a Group root before; you've gone to church and you've done that but you've never had people who actually knew you and loved you. Maybe today you're going to take that step. Maybe you've been part of a group before and now you're going to take it a level deeper. You're going to be devoted to people and to prayer and to sharing Jesus with one another. I don't know what your next step is, but I pray that you take it because I know in time you won't regret it. A pineapple takes 13 to 16 months to grow, and your Group root might take just as long. But I guarantee that if you commit yourself, it will be just as good.

I hope you think about your faith that way. I know there are so many things to keep you busy in the moment, but I'm not thinking about the in-the-moment you. I'm thinking about the six-months-from-now you. I'm thinking about the two-years-from-now you. I'm thinking about the decade-from-now you. I'm thinking about your children and grandchildren connected to you. I want you and them to enjoy good fruit.

Plant a root, plant a seed, and pray for it to grow.

So plant a root, plant a seed, and pray for it to grow. Do you want more love, more peace, more joy, more fruit? Then I know your next step: Get a group!

Your Group Root

The fruit of the Spirit is love, joy, peace, forbearance, kindness, goodness, faithfulness, gentleness, and self control.
Galatians 5:22,23

Want ____________? Get a ______________!

They devoted themselves to the apostles' teaching and to fellowship, to the breaking of bread and to prayer.
Acts 2:42

4 Keys to a good group:

1. Devoted to the __________ __________.
2. Devoted to _________________.
3. Devoted to the _______ ____ ________.
4. Devoted to _________________.

Points to Ponder

1. Read the apostle Peter's teaching in Acts 2:14–41. Name at least three of Peter's main points. How do those points affect the way you want to do group today?

2. Evaluate the current strength of your Group root. What small step could you take to strengthen that root so that your future might include more spiritual fruit?

Roots
GATHER GROUP GROW GIVE GO

Gather Together

"So, Pastor, why do I still have to go to church?" A couple of weeks ago, a high school senior from my ministry, a young man who had been raised in an incredible family, had the courage to call me up and ask that honest question. "Pastor, why would I still go to church?" And he gave me permission to share the conversation here.

Why do I still have to go to church?

He said that he and a bunch of his classmates who had attended a Christian school for years, teenagers who had grown up going to church every Sunday, were all asking this question: "Why our freshman year or throughout our college years would we keep going to church?" He said not a single guy in that circle could come up with a compelling answer.

This young man had heard me talk many times in our church about the rooted tree picture that we love to put up. He had heard that if you want spiritual fruit in your life, such as love for people or joy in your connection to God or peace with your conscience or self-control against sin, you need strong roots: Gather, Group, Grow, Give, and Go. But his honest question for me was around the Gather root: "Does it really, Pastor? If I really want peace with God and joy in my life and self-control against temptation, do I have to gather?" He said, "My classmates and I realize we've been hearing this same stuff for years, and our teachers tell us we should keep going to church to grow in faith, but we've heard everything. So why would we still go?"

You know, I give that young man an incredible amount of credit for being humble and honest enough to ask his pastor that question. It's a good question because if you haven't had to wrestle with it, you will, or someone you care very much about will wrestle with it. If you're a teenager, the time is coming when Mom and Dad won't be able to tell you what to do. When you get your own place or go off to campus, you'll have to decide if it's still worth it to go to church. If you go to church to hear your kids sing or if you're at church with your boyfriend or girlfriend, you're going to have to wrestle with that question: "Well, why would I come back?" Or if you aren't going to church for some reason and perhaps watch *Time of Grace* on TV or listen to a podcast, you're going to have to wrestle with that question too: "If God gives me the health and strength to attend a church next Sunday, why would I go?"

I think that in modern times it's actually a better question than ever. People are busy. If your profession is anything like mine, it's busier than ever before. About 50 years ago, the U.S. government predicted that advances in technology would mean that the average U.S. citizen would work about 20 hours a week. If you haven't figured it out, they were dead wrong. We work and work and work, and the 40-hour workweek for many people is a thing of the past. We spend 50 hours in the office, and then we bring our phones home and return emails in bed on Saturdays and Sundays. Sometimes there's only a little time on the weekend to unplug and relax. Going to church is hard.

A generation ago, it used to be that Sunday was a sacred day, an untouchable day, but no longer. Not if you want your kid to play varsity sports; he or she has got to start in club, and club doesn't take Sundays off. So there are tournaments and commitments. We scramble throughout the weekends, and sometimes Sundays are the only time to get stuff done around the house. Sometimes we're exhausted, our friends are in town, or we're having a good time, and going to church is hard or busy. Not only that, perhaps now more than

It's easy to replace what happens at church in the comfort of our own homes.

ever, it's easy to replace what happens at church in the comfort of our own homes.

Now, I realize that you can do almost all of the five roots without being in a church. With the rise of social media, you don't need to gather at church to find a spiritual community. You can connect, post Bible passages, pray for one another, and encourage each other digitally without stepping foot in a church. And you can grow! You can listen to sermons in the comfort of your own home. You can podcast me at double speed so it's over in half the time. You can open the YouVersion Bible app and do devotions, and you can watch other preachers and different music on YouTube without stepping foot in a church. You can go online and give electronically, and you can go and share your faith with a thousand people without being in a church.

Five hundred years ago when people didn't have Bibles in their homes, it might have seemed like a necessity to go to a place of worship where the book was chained to the church, but not anymore. We have 24/7 access. So the question this kid asked me was a good one: "Do I have to? Is church just a nice thing for people if it works out? Or is it really a necessity in my spiritual life? Do I have to have that root to produce all this spiritual fruit?"

Before I share with you what I shared with that young man before he left for his freshman year of college, I want to dive into one chapter of the Bible that gives us three solid answers to that question—Why gather? Let's travel back about three thousand years to the ancient songbook of the Bible, the book of Psalms, to a time when God inspired an anonymous author to give us great reasons to gather together.

Psalm 92 is smack dab in the middle of your Bible, and it begins in a really interesting way: **"A psalm. A song. For the Sabbath day."** There are 150 songs in the book of Psalms, but this is the only one that begins with that specific title: **"For the Sabbath day."** If you know much about the first pages of the Bible, you might remember that *Sabbath* is a Hebrew word that means “rest.” When God gave the Ten Commandments to his people, when he rescued them from their slavery in Egypt, he commanded them to remember the Sabbath day by keeping it holy. He didn’t suggest it; he ordered them to take one day, Saturday, every week to rest. No going to work and no returning emails on your tablets or however you did it back then. He said, “I want you to rest. I want you to gather with the people whom you love, and I want you to remember. I want you to gather and remind each other of the God who gave you rest. I am the God who created you and rested on the seventh day. I am the God who rescued you from Egypt so you wouldn’t have to work 24/7 for your slave master. I gave you a chance to breathe because you’re forgiven and loved and redeemed.” What’s interesting is that throughout the entire history of the Bible, from start to finish, that’s what God’s people did. They gathered on the Sabbath. Throughout the Old Testament, every Saturday they would pause their schedules and gather together in God's name. Even in between the Old and New Testaments, people were scattered to all different nations. They invented something because they couldn't all gather in Jerusalem to worship. It was called a synagogue. *Synagogue* is a word that literally means "to gather together."

By the time the New Testament came around and we read about Jesus, it says he went to the synagogue **"as was his custom"** (Luke 4:16). Jesus was in the habit, the custom, of gathering with others to hear the Word of God and to sing praises. The rest of the New Testament gives us proof. The reason your New Testament is so long with books like Romans and Corinthians and Galatians and Ephesians and Philippians and Thessalonians is because God's people gathered. For thousands of years, they got

Jesus was in the habit, the custom, of gathering together to hear the Word of God and to sing praises.

into the habit of gathering for worship on a weekly basis. Sometimes it was on Saturday; for some of the New Testament Christians, it was Sunday to remember the day of Jesus' resurrection. Sometimes it was in a church or in house churches. Sometimes it was at the temple in Jerusalem. For all of history, God's people got into this habit. They gathered.

But the question remains: *Why?* Why did God command it? Why was it Jesus' custom to do it, and why did Peter and Paul and all the people who came to follow Jesus follow in those footsteps? That's what the rest of this psalm is going to answer for you and me. We're going to find in this psalm three powerful reasons to gather and to keep gathering together into the future.

"It is good to praise the LORD and make music to your name, O Most High, proclaiming your love in the morning and your faithfulness at night, to the music of the ten-stringed lyre and the melody of the harp. For you make me glad by your deeds, LORD; I sing for joy

at what your hands had done. How great are your works, Lord, how profound your thoughts!" (Psalm 92:1–5). The psalmist says it's good to praise and proclaim to the music of the ten-stringed lyre. He talks about the melody of the harp, and he sings for joy. So the first compelling reason that he gives is so we can sing together. Because there's something powerful about music, isn't there? Five hundred years ago, the reformer Martin Luther said that the second best gift that God has given to humankind after the Bible is music; we're wired to enjoy music. Your genre and your style might vary, your radio station might not be the same as mine, but there's something powerful about music. It's true for out there in the world, and it's also true for the people of God.

Two or three weeks ago, I met with a woman from my church family who's going through a pretty tough time in her life with her family and relationships. And she talked to me about how much it meant to gather at church week after week. At one point she said, "Pastor, no offense, your messages are nice, but the music!" I wasn't offended one bit because I often feel the same way. Sometimes a sermon hits home, but sometimes if the sermon misses the mark, it's the songs that get to our hearts. It's why preschool teachers like my wife turn everything into a jingle or a song, because music makes things memorable and buries them deep. My daughter and I were singing a random song about adverbs and adjectives and verbs in our van last week. She might have never remembered the English lesson, but since it was put in a song, she remembers what all those things mean. How powerful is that when it comes to sin and grace? How amazing, as the psalmist says, when we can sing not just about the things of this world but about the love and the faithfulness of God? When we can talk about spiritual things and put them to music, it has a profound effect. In fact, what happens is fruit is produced.

What happens when we sing?

Remember that passage from Galatians about the fruit of the Spirit? Three of the nine fruits are love, faithfulness, and joy. What happens when we sing? The Holy Spirit produces these fruits.

If you're a more logical thinker, you might realize that I haven't exactly answered my original question: Why go to church? Feeling the power of music and singing the praises of God are things you could do at home, couldn't you? The answer's yes. We call that the Grow root (more on that next chapter!), but there's still something powerful about gathering together and singing together. In fact, let me prove it to you. Why is it that some people battle crowds and wait in line and pay $40 or $60 or $100 or more for good tickets to a favorite band? Is the band going to play some shocking new music that they've never heard before? Nope. They could listen to all their favorite songs for free, and they wouldn't have to leave the comfort of their couches. So why do it? Because part of music's power is what happens when people sing it together, when it's not just you singing in the car or not just you singing in the shower. When there are dozens, hundreds, or thousands of voices joined together, there is power in song.

You've experienced that, right? Have you ever been to a church service where nobody shows up because of a snowstorm or something and there's maybe six people scattered throughout church? It's really awkward when you sing, right? But have you ever been to a service when everyone sings? People sing out, and there's something about the energy in the room that takes your emotions and your heart to another level. When I go to church and get to sit way up in the front, sometimes in the middle of a song I'll stop singing and listen. There's something powerful about hearing others sing about the love and the joy and the faithfulness and the works and the words of God. There's something incredible about hearing the voices of kids, and when I hear my sisters in the faith shamelessly belting the words of the God who saved them, it's powerful. Isn't there something when guys sing too? We guys don't sing over a lot of things, but there's something powerful about a bunch of dudes who shamelessly lift up the cross in the name of Jesus Christ. That's why we gather.

By myself I might forget how powerful the name of God is, but when we lift up our voices together and remind each other how great he is, there are ten thousand reasons to bless the Lord because of his reckless, crazy love for us. When every voice joins in song, there is incredible power.

So here's the psalmist's first argument: Why do we gather? Because to gather is music—it produces love, faithfulness, and joy, which are three of the nine fruits of the Spirit.

The psalmist continues in the second stanza of Psalm 92 with these words: **"Senseless people do not know, fools do not understand, that though the wicked spring up like grass and all evildoers flourish, they will be destroyed forever. But you, Lord, are forever exalted. For surely your**

enemies, Lord, surely your enemies will perish; all evildoers will be scattered. You have exalted my horn like that of a wild ox; fine oils have been poured on me. My eyes have seen the defeat of my adversaries; my ears have heard the rout of my wicked foes" (verses 6–11).

This gets intense, doesn't it? In the first stanza of the psalm there's music and joy and love and faithfulness, but then the psalmist comes back in the second stanza with evildoers, enemies, wicked foes, and adversaries. I count seven to eight times in these few verses that he talks about those who oppose the kingdom and the name of God. But I'm glad he wrote it because there are people who do not support the name of Jesus, and they don't live out the love of Jesus. Sometimes, as he says in verse 6, they seem to spring up and flourish. Go to your job, walk the average high school hallway, look at those who are popular and powerful; it's not always the people who show love to others or who love the God of love who flourish. Sometimes it's the arrogant athlete at high school who gets all the girls' attention, but the young man who loves God and humbly tries to serve him gets totally forgotten. Sometimes it's the mean skinny girls who gossip and spend way too much time in front of a mirror who turn heads as they walk down the hallway, while the young woman who's so passionate about Jesus and faithful in prayer isn't asked to the homecoming dance. Sometimes it's the politician who lies and covers up who ends up in a position of power, while justice is trampled on and good people suffer.

It happens to you too, doesn't it? Maybe you're going through a divorce and you try to be humble and admit to the judge in the courtroom that it wasn't totally one-sided; there were some things that you did wrong. And what does your ex do? He and his lawyer pounce on the information and spin it, and you suffer in profound ways because of your honesty. Evil flourishes. Some of you want the comment section to be a place of honest dialogue online, so you try to be meek and humble and try to seek first to understand. It's the people who leave the caps lock on and blow it up that get all the attention. Or you go to a job interview and try to be an honest person; you don't just have the strengths listed on your résumé. You also have some honest weaknesses that you want your employer to know about. But it's the person who fakes it and acts like a perfect employee who gets the job ahead of you. Sometimes you do the right thing and don't win. Sometimes nice guys don't finish first.

What does this psalmist know though? That even though evildoers might flourish, in the end only God will be exalted. In the end, all the wicked will be scattered, and God and his faithful people will triumph. God knows that lies will not win and racism will not win and bigotry and hate will not win and injustice will not win. When everything is done, when the score is finally settled, only Jesus and his people will win. Which is one of the many reasons the psalmist gathered with others.

You probably know that one of the ugliest parts of America's history is when evildoers flourished by breaking the backs of God's black sons and daughters. Read the history, and you will find that some white plantation owners who said they were Christian opened Bibles and forced their slaves to come and worship. They would take passages, twist them out of context, and wicked preachers would tell them that kidnapping, racism, torture, abuse, and oppression were actually the will of God. But do you know what happened after the sermon was over? Many of those slaves would gather. When the master wasn't there to twist the Scriptures, they would gather and remember the stories they heard about the God of the Bible. The God who once saved his enslaved people in Egypt. The God who said that justice would roll like a river. The God of Dr. King and so many like him who lifted up people who were oppressed and victims of injustice and told them that judgment is coming. Evildoers might spring up, but in the end, only God will be exalted. There in broken-down, old cabins, they sang Negro spirituals. They gathered together. They reminded one another that evil will not win. They reminded one another to be faithful and endure to the end because he who stands firm will be saved.

I pray you never have to go through abuse like that, but you know what it's like to do the right thing and not be rewarded. To stand up for Jesus and not be applauded. To try to choose the path of righteousness and everyone accuses you of wrongdoing. That's where Psalm 92 is golden. When you gather together in a church, you remind one another what might have been forgotten out in the world. After six days of headlines, of spin and politics, of drama and racism and injustice, we might think that evil will have the last word. But when you gather with others you say, "No, no, no. Only Jesus. Our hope, our future, is in Jesus. One day oppression will end. One day Jesus will return. One day every wickedness will be called into account, and every person who has suffered for the name of God will be exalted." As we remind each other of this, what happens? Peace. Patience to suffer another day with faithfulness. The psalmist would say that we gather together because gatherers produce patience and peace.

We gather together because gatherers produce patience and peace.

Finally, in the last words of the psalm, the psalmist gives perhaps his best words of all: **"The righteous will flourish like a palm tree, they will grow like a cedar of Lebanon; planted in the house of the Lord, they will flourish in the courts of our God. They will still bear fruit in old age, they will stay fresh and green, proclaiming, 'The Lord is upright; he is my Rock, and there is no wickedness in him'"** (verses 12–15).

We flourish and we grow and we flourish again, and we bear fruit and we stay fresh and we stay green and we find that we have this Rock. We become like a cedar of Lebanon. Do you know what that means? Even today like in biblical times, the cedar trees in Lebanon grow tall and last a long time there. Some are 100 feet tall, and some of them are over a thousand years old, the very cedars that built the temple in Jerusalem in the days of Solomon. That's what you become when you gather.

It happens in the house of the Lord, in the courts of our God. And if you are an older Christian, notice when? Still in old age, we stay fresh and green. The metabolism slows, and the weight starts to creep up. The salt overtakes the pepper, but you can still be fresh in the eyes of God. If you're planted in his promises, you can still have peace and joy in your life even if your best days seem to be behind you. Did you notice why? Because as old and young gather together, we proclaim the Lord is upright; he is our Rock.

There's an old hymn that says, "On Christ the solid rock I stand; all other ground is shifting sand." Do you ever notice that when you leave church everything is like shifting sand? You thought you were going to do that this week, and then it shifts on you. You thought your boss was going to tell you this, and then she shifted on you. You thought your health was like this, and it shifted on you. There are so many "what ifs" and "what abouts" that you can never be certain; you can never have that fruit of peace in your life—until you remember that God is your Rock. Jesus made a promise to you that he would live a perfect life in your place, and he did. He died on a cross so you and I wouldn't have to live with a scarlet letter on our chests. He promised that he would conquer death so that if you're close to death you don't have to be afraid of it, and he did. He promised he would ascend to the right hand of God and would rule your city, block, street, zip code, and home for the good of his church, and he is. Out there, there's nothing that's certain, and no wonder you and I live with anxiety and fear. But when we gather together, we remind each other there is a Messiah, a Christ, named Jesus and he is faithful to every promise he has made.

So what do we learn from the final verses? That gatherers produce fruit: peace and joy and love and faithfulness. That's why we gather. That's why I hope you go back to church. That's why I hope if you haven't gone to church before, you go for the first time.

That's what Leticia told me. Leticia is one of the many incredible people who serve on my sermon research team. Every time I preach, I send questions and bounce ideas off about ten people from my church. They give me new things to think about, new perspectives, and I asked our sermon research team about this: Why do you do this? Here's what Leticia said: "Not being at church feels empty and wrong. Not in a guilt-type sense, but in the most important part of the week is missing kind of way." I love that! It's not because some preacher is twisting your arm or beating you over the head with a Bible. It's because you don't want to miss a chance to remember how incredible God is!

Here's what Leticia said next: "I like

to be like a squirrel in church. I'll bite and hoard all of the fruit inside my cheeks for a later date." That is an incredible quote. You know, sometimes the message doesn't get you right away, but you never know what's going to happen tomorrow. Sometimes the song doesn't give you incredible peace in the moment, but it will come into your mind on Wednesday when that unexpected news hits. Like spiritual squirrels, we stuff as much Jesus into our cheeks because we know sometime during the week we are desperately going to need him.

So what's your next step? Maybe it's to find a church that lifts up the name of Jesus, and once you find that church you will get connected. Maybe you already have a church, and for the first time in your life you're going to decide that your day of worship is the Sabbath that you will keep holy. Instead of figuring out next weekend if you're too busy to go, it'll be a rock-solid part of your schedule because you believe that you would miss something really important if you weren't in church.

What if you go to church every Sunday? What's your next step? Here's one idea: What if you studied the words of one song before you went? Music can move your heart and become your favorite tune, but if you don't actually stop and read the words, you've missed about 90 percent of what the author is trying to communicate. What if you found out what music would be playing at your church in the next service. You could pick one song, go online and read the lyrics, and really think about the meaning so that when you sing it later, you will be singing from your heart, not just reading words.

> *This Gather root ...will produce incredible fruit.*

I don't know what your next step is, but I know this: This Gather root, if you give it enough time, will produce incredible fruit. And that's what I told that 18-year-old. Remember him from the beginning of this chapter? "Pastor, why should I keep going to church?" Here's my answer: "You know, you're right. You know a lot about Christianity, but Christianity isn't just about what you know. It's about how you love." Jesus said the two most important things for a human being would be to love God with his or her whole heart and to love every single human being, every neighbor, as themselves. I told that teen, "You have no clue how many things will compete for first place in your heart. You have no clue how many things—popularity or money or privilege or status or career—will fight to take the throne from Jesus in your heart. You have no clue how hard it's going to be to love, to be on campus with Christians and atheists, with Muslims and Buddhists, with LGBTQs and pansexuals. How hard it will be to live with people who love the church and hate those who hate it, with men and women, with young and old, with Republican and Democrat and Libertarian and everything else. You have no clue how hard it will be to love everyone as much as you love yourself. So, man, here's what I'm going to tell you—if you want that kind of fruit, don't forget about the root. Your mom and dad have given you 18 years of roots in the gospel of Jesus Christ, and so if you have any faith, it's because of that. Don't uproot yourself and expect the same amount of fruit. If you're ready to have faith and joy and love next year like you have this year, keep your roots."

That young man is at school now. I pray that watching *Time of Grace* on TV or listening to our podcast isn't his only connection to Jesus. I pray today and next week and next month he's planted in the house of God. Because those who are planted in the house of God will flourish. Even into old age, they will bear fruit. If you want more fruit, don't forget about this Gather root.

Your Gather Root

Psalm 92

A Psalm. A Song. For the Sabbath Day.

3 Reasons to Gather:

1. Psalm 92:1–5:
   Gatherer's music produces ________, __________, and __________.

2. Psalm 92:6–11: In the end, gatherers produce __________ and ____________.

3. Psalm 92:12–15: Gatherers remind each other that we have a ______________.

Points to Ponder

1. Read Hebrews 10:19–25. What habit were some of the early Christians getting into? How does the author of Hebrews try to persuade them to recommit themselves to gathering in Jesus' name?

2. If your best friends believed they didn't need a church family to follow Jesus personally, what would you say to convince them otherwise? What Bible passages would you turn to in order to make your point more than your own personal opinion?

3. What is your next step to strengthen your Gather root? To put church in your calendar as a repeating event that you will protect in your schedule? To read/study the Scriptures and songs before you arrive on Sunday? Other? Whatever your plan, share it with a trusted Christian friend and ask him or her to ask God to bless it!

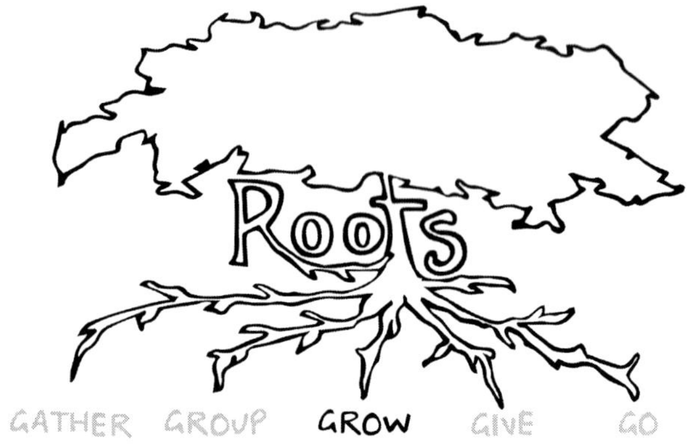
Roots
GATHER GROUP GROW GIVE GO

Grow Closer to Jesus

GQ magazine recently published an article entitled, "21 Books You Don't Have to Read." Guess what book made their list? The Bible. Which seems pretty crazy because it's the best-selling book of all time; and whether you're a Christian or an atheist, you have to admit it's a book that has changed world history and American culture more than any other. I didn't agree with the total article, but there's a line in the article that caught my attention. Jesse Ball, who wrote his review of the Bible, included these words: "The Holy Bible is rated very highly by all the people who supposedly live by it but who in actuality have not read it." There's some truth to that.

People in the church world love this book and regard it highly. In fact, we believe it's holy because it comes from the Holy Spirit. It was actually written by God, many Christians believe, and given through human authors. But despite our belief in it and our esteem of it, if your life is anything like mine, we don't always find time to read it. The Bible is a challenge to read, and many Christians go days, weeks, months, and years without making reading it a habit in their daily lives.

If you've ever been there, or maybe you're there right now, I totally get it. I know it's a pastor thing to say things like, "We should all read our Bibles every single day." But when I think about that, what it must be like for you to hear that, I get why so much time can go by without opening it. I mean, when is the last time you read a book that big? The Bible's a massive book, and not everyone loves to snuggle up with a good book on a rainy day. Some of us love to read, and some of us don't. So to read anything, much less a book of this magnitude, seems crazy.

Not only that, the Bible isn't a book

written by modern people in modern times. The most recent parts of it were written 1,900 years ago. Some of its parts were written by Moses 3,500 years ago; there's poetry and prophecy by ancient Hebrew people, and it can be really difficult to understand. I went to school for a lot of years to study the Bible, and there are some parts that I read and think to myself, "What in the world does that mean?" So if you're brand-new to church or you've been around just a few years, I could encourage you to read the Bible, but you would open its pages and be thoroughly baffled by many of them.

That's not the only thing. The more complicating factor is that like me, your life is busy. You're not just sitting around with dozens of extra hours during your week. You might have a job or family commitments; you might be raising small kids or working mandatory overtime. You might have tons on your plate with friendships or taking care of aging parents. To really grasp and get a lot out of the Bible, it's going to take some quiet, quantity time, and you probably don't have a lot of it.

This chapter is all about the Grow root. I learned something else from that tree root article that I read the other day. Thomas Perry said the number-one thing that prevents roots from thriving and growing is soil compaction. He said if there's a lot of foot traffic around the trunk of a tree, it will actually compact the soil so much and make it so dense that there isn't a lot of space and room for the roots to grow. That's kind of a perfect picture of life, right? We run from work to school to extracurriculars to kids' stuff to friends to birthday parties for our little sister or our second cousin. Life goes at this frantic pace, and it compacts our schedules so much that we don't have the breathing room that the Bible requires. Actually, your parents might appreciate that Dr. Perry found out

To really grasp and get a lot out of the Bible, it's going to take some quiet, quantity time.

that the kind of feet that can compact the soil the most are little feet. Even though kids don't weigh as much, apparently their feet are smaller and there's more pressure per square inch. So if you have kids running around the tree that you call life, by the time you put them to bed, you collapse without a lot of mental energy to open this ancient book and get a lot out of it.

So here I am another pastor who's going to tell you the same, old thing that pastors have been saying for who knows how long—you should really read your Bible. You shouldn't just go to church and gather in God's name. Every day, you should try to grow closer to Jesus. However, I realize if that's pretty challenging for me as a pastor, it's equally challenging for you. Often, I'm tempted to help you figure out the *how*. You know, here's how you do it. I could pass out a double-sided worksheet that tells you to read this part of the Bible

The how doesn't do you much good unless you have a convincing why.

on this day, check the box, and then answer these two questions, but I've come to realize after many years that the *how* doesn't do you much good unless you have a convincing *why*.

Why would you even do this? If this is going to be really hard to read, why would you battle through it the first time? Why would you stop doing the stuff that brings you instant joy, like scrolling through social media, put your phone down, and pick the Bible up? Why would you do that? Why would you commit yourself for the next year to reading a book that you might get a lot out of or maybe you won't, as I try to convince you this is worth reading every day for the rest of your life? Why would you change your habits and your schedule to make space for this book?

That's the question I want to tackle here. Yes, I'm going to give you a little bit of the *how*. But I want to spend the bulk of this chapter on giving you a convincing *why*. Why is this worth it if it can be so difficult for modern, busy people?

Thankfully, I don't have to answer the *why* question by myself because there was a guy who lived about six hundred years before Jesus was born named Jeremiah. In his Bible book, which is very complex and poetic and prophetic, he gives us this really great reason to be people who have a constant and daily connection to the Word of God. Here's a roadmap of where we're going to go. We're going to look at just four or five verses from the book of Jeremiah, and Jeremiah's going to paint poetically the picture of the kind of spiritual person you don't want to be, and he's going to tell you the kind of spiritual person all of us want to be. Then he's going to explain why the Bible is the one thing that can move you from one kind of person to another kind of person.

Are you ready to see why the Bible is not just the best-selling book but the best book of all time? Here's Jeremiah 17:5,6: **"This is what the Lord says: 'Cursed is the one who trusts in man, who draws strength from mere flesh and whose heart turns away from the Lord. That person will be like a**

bush in the wastelands; they will not see prosperity when it comes. They will dwell in the parched places of the desert, in a salt land where no one lives.'"

This is classic Jeremiah. He doesn't come out bluntly and say, "Not reading the Bible is bad." Instead, he uses poetry to paint this picture. Maybe you felt the emotion of it. He's describing someone who is spiritually cursed and not blessed. He says it's like that person's parched; it's like his soul is crawling on elbows and knees through this dry, salty, deserted place. Jeremiah pictures this cottonmouth and thick tongue and cracked lips depiction of the soul that you would not want to have. Did you catch who he says ends up in a place like that? The one whose confidence and trust is in man. **"Cursed is the one who trusts in man, who draws strength from mere flesh and whose heart turns away from the Lord."** He says what happens to us is that if we simply put our trust in man, we can often end up in a spot that none of us would choose. In other words, if we try to figure out what will make us blessed or what will make us cursed, if the final vote in those huge discussions for our souls comes down to any man or any woman instead of God, eventually our hearts will turn from God and end up cursed. That "man" could be any man or woman. If our trust is in what our mom or dad told us, what our pastor or priest said, what our favorite professor or our peers say, what a pop star or the polls tell us. If we look to our feelings, our emotions, our thoughts, our intuitions, our hearts, our guts, or let our consciences be our guides, then we trust in man. Jeremiah says we end up spiritually in a place that we don't want to be.

If you leave a thing to itself, it gets worse and not better.

The reason why, according to Jeremiah, is because the law of entropy applies to our hearts. Have you ever heard of that before, the law of entropy? It's a fancy scientific theory that essentially says this: A closed system tends toward disorder and chaos.

Here's another way to say it: If you leave a thing to itself, it gets worse and not better. The law of entropy is what I saw last Friday when I looked at my garden. My family's been kind of busy; my wife normally takes care of our garden every few days and waters it, but she's been busy teaching three- and four-year-olds so she hasn't been back in the garden. And to be honest, I've been terrified of the mosquitoes, so I haven't been anywhere near it for about two weeks. But then I mowed my yard and took a first pass where I could finally see the little garden behind the shed, and do you want to guess what I found? It was cursed. The garden was not thriving; there was one gigantic zucchini but mostly weeds. The tomatoes had fallen off the cages, and they were cracked and broken in the soil. It was weedy; I couldn't tell the difference between what was good and what needed to be ripped up and thrown into the garbage pile. In other words, we left the garden by itself, and it didn't get better; it got worse.

According to Jeremiah, the same thing

happens to the human heart. If God doesn't have a chance to garden it, to prune what's going well so it can thrive and to pull out the sin that would choke out a thriving faith, it will not get better; it will get worse. If all we have is human opinion, trying to grow together closer to God, our faith doesn't end up in the place we thought it would. The cursed, the spiritually unhappy, trust in man. And I'm totally aware that if you're under the age of let's say 30, that seems crazy. You might not know this if you're in your 20s or you're a teenager, but you've grown up in a culture that tells you the opposite of what Jeremiah's saying. You can probably finish these sentences, right? "You need to trust your ______." "You should follow your ______." "Your intuition wouldn't ______ to you." "You can ______ your feelings." That's all we hear: "Be true to yourself." "It's outside people, institutions, and authority that are the problem. The truth is found within you."

However, not everyone for human history has believed that. In fact, God, when he spoke to Jeremiah, said that we shouldn't believe that. It's in the same chapter of Jeremiah that we find this in verse 9: **"The heart,"** my heart and your heart, **"is deceitful above all things and beyond cure. Who can understand it?"** He's saying that the heart is deceitful. We can talk ourselves into anything; we are the best salespeople for bad ideas for ourselves. If God doesn't speak to us from the outside, we will not end up closer to him but farther away. It's kind of what King Josiah learned; do you recognize that name from the Bible? He lived right about the time of Jeremiah. Josiah became king of the southern part of Israel when he was eight years old. The Bible says that when he turned about 26, in the 18th year of his reign, he decided to pull an HGTV and remodel the temple in Jerusalem. He hired craftsmen and artisans and workmen; they were going to clean out the old temple and make it beautiful again. But as they cleaned it out, they found this book inside the dusty temple. They blew the dust off the cover and found out that the book was the Bible. They brought it to King Josiah, who was a fairly good king by comparison when it came to worshiping the true God, and one of the members of his court started reading the book, the words of God. When King Josiah heard it, he wept. The Bible says he actually took his royal robes and ripped them apart. He was so grieved that he and his family thought they were so close to God, but it turned out they had drifted so far.

That's what God wants to spare you from. He doesn't want you to find out a year from now that the way you've been dating or thinking of your sexuality or marriage is far, far, far from what God intends. He doesn't want five years of family life to go by before you get blindsided thinking that you really didn't understand what love and patience and forgiveness look like. He doesn't want you to look back on your life ten years from now and realize that the things that God takes very seriously you thought were just being human and not serious at all. And he doesn't want you on your deathbed living with guilt and shame and fear because you never realized that when God says he loves you with no strings attached, he means it. See, Jeremiah knows that if God does not speak to us, we will not get anything right. We won't take sin very seriously. We won't grasp forgiveness with its power and its punch. We won't figure out what marriage or gender or religion or authority or church or faith or anything else is about because the heart deceives us.

As I'm writing this, I'm thinking that's my entire case for you to read the Bible. There are a thousand arguments a pastor could make, but it all really comes down to this. If your heart is capable of doing life with God's blessing without this book, I don't think you'll read it. I think you'll be too busy, and it will be too complex. If you trust and have confidence that you're going to figure life out, you won't have the motivation to open the Bible. But if you actually believe what God is saying through Jeremiah—that your heart will deceive you—then, man, things will get messed up really fast unless God speaks to you. Then you will have the passion to say, "I can't make a decision. I can't go back to my job. I can't do life in this country. I can't do life God's way unless he speaks to me and tells me what his way is."

Here's a straightforward question for you: Do you believe what God says about your heart? Do you believe it is as deceptive and tricky and lies to you as often as it does? If your answer to that question is yes, God is ready to speak to you because your Father in heaven doesn't just want to make you busier; he isn't giving you this book so you can read it a lot and earn his love. No, like a good Father, he wants you to listen to his voice so that you will be blessed. In fact, that's what Jeremiah says next.

He says, **"But blessed is the one who trusts in the Lord; whose confidence is in him"** (verse 7). See the contrast? **"They will be like a tree planted by the water that sends out its roots by the stream. It does not fear when heat comes; its leaves are**

always green. It has no worries in a year of drought and never fails to bear fruit” (verse 8). I love, love those words. My wife, about a month ago, wrote those two verses on this big chalkboard door that sits in our kitchen. Every day my family sees it, and it’s so beautiful and so clear: Blessed is the one who trusts in God. God says if you trust in him, if you’re like a tree planted by the water, he will come and the difficult season of life might arrive like a drought and yet, what? You don’t have to worry, and you will never fail to bear fruit.

You don’t have to worry, and you will never fail to bear fruit.

God is saying if you read his Word, life might not get easier. There will still be tragedy and cancer and death and depression and anxiety and mental illness and addiction. Opening the Bible once won’t erase a craving for drugs or alcohol or pornography; it doesn’t work that way. But what God says is that in the middle of the craziness of life, you will never fail to bear fruit. That there will still be love and peace and joy, and I love the little details why. Because if you're in God's Word every day, you will be like a tree planted by the water.

You know what the problem is with the trees in my yard? They're not by water. They're totally dependent on rainstorms or a sprinkler. That's kind of like a Christian who only goes to church. His or her faith is totally dependent on how good or not good the Sunday message is. But what would happen if you were a tree planted by the water? Every single day, your soul had access to the source of life and it had access to Jesus? Well, then I could flop it; I could preach the worst sermon in the world and your soul wouldn't shrivel and dry up for another week because you would have six or seven days of constant access to the Word of God.

If you want to be blessed, then plant your soul, your life, by the source of life.

See, this is Jeremiah's point: If you want to be blessed, then plant your soul, your life, by the source of life—the Word of God. Then you can end up like a guy I met on another continent named Micah. I heard about Micah and his wife, Kayla, long before I visited Thailand. They're coworkers, and some of their superiors in the missionary organization they were a part of said these two were a force of nature for Jesus. They would go into a city where very few people were gathering in Jesus' name, and they would love people so well and invest in them so passionately and have such peace and joy in their relationship with God that when they would open the Word, the city would get changed. Then they would leave. They were like this force of nature that would leave a wake of gospel love behind them. I was very curious to meet them, and when I did, Micah told me the most interesting story. He said that he had grown up in a Christian church, and it was a good church. He was raised by Christian parents, and they were really solid Christian parents. He went to a Christian school, and it didn't scar him and wasn't hypocritical; it was a solid school that lifted up the name of Jesus. But Micah confessed to me that not once in his entire life did he open the Bible for himself. His teachers would tell him he had to read this story or memorize this verse, and he would. They would schedule chapel on this day of the week, and he would go. His parents would wake him up to bring him to church, and he would attend, but it was always something he was forced to do and not something that he chose to do.

But when he ended up in a different country, Micah realized that he needed help. So, he desperately turned to the Word. He told me that when he did, his faith—which was strong to begin with—exploded in all the right ways. He found more joy in Jesus. He found more peace than ever before. He found more of a commitment to love people with faithfulness and hospitality and kindness. I remember well when he said, "I never did it before, but now that I have, I'm not going back."

Your story could be like his. Maybe you

went to a Christian school, maybe you've been going to church for a long time, or maybe you've only been to church once. I don't know your story, but I know this: If your connection is not just week by week or school year by school year but day by day, you will find something powerful. Here's why. I would summarize it this way—why would you grow? What did my friend Micah find? My one-word answer is *Jesus*.

The Bible is not just about ancient poetry and prophecy; it's a book about Jesus. If you meet the real Jesus in the pages of that book, it must change you. It has to. I mean, how would it be possible that you could meet Jesus, the God of love, in this book and not end up wanting to love people in return? The Bible says that Jesus is so committed to you that while you were still a sinner, he died for you. It says that no matter what a wreck this past week was, that God's love is still full and free for you. This book says that if you've been sober for five years or you haven't been sober for five minutes, that God is still forgiving and kind and is pleased with you because of what Jesus has done. The Bible says that you don't have to earn God's love, and you don't deserve it or merit it. You don't take steps up a ladder to get to him. It says that God is so full of love that Jesus climbed down the ladder to get to you. If you would meet a God like that who loves you more than your parents, your boyfriend, your girlfriend, your children, anyone in the world, how could that love not sink deep into your heart like a seed and produce something beautiful? Or how could you read about the Jesus in this book and not have joy?

> *The God who knows all of your messes . . . rejoices in you.*

One of my favorite things about the Jesus of the Bible is that he doesn't just put up with me, and he doesn't just accept you. The Bible says because he took away every one of our sins on the cross, he delights in us. Do you believe that? The God who knows all of your messes, the whole story, smiles and laughs and rejoices in you. God is so committed because of what Jesus did that he took every sin to the cross and gave you every bit of the perfect life that he lived. God thinks of you and rejoices. He kicks open the front gates of heaven and throws open his arms wide and loves you. If you believe that, how could that not give you a bit of joy?

If you would meet the Jesus of the Bible, how could you not have peace? You know the thing you're worried about right now? The struggle in your family, the anxiety at work, the mental illness, the addiction, the court date, that thing—do you know where that is? Underneath the feet of Jesus. Jesus kicks up his feet like a footstool on your worries. He's not losing sleep over them. Jesus isn't worried about who the president is or who's going to sit on the bench of the Supreme Court. Jesus holds all things in the palm of his hand. They're totally under his control. Our God who loves us is in total control of the universe. If you remember that while you're lying in bed at night, how could you not just take a deep breath and have peace?

Why read the Bible? Because this book reminds you that Jesus is not a small, sandal-wearing, sappy Savior. He is the King of kings and Lord of lords; he is full of power and love, and he loves you.

That's what Zack's mom told him. I read this really great book last year called the *Imperfect Pastor* by a pastor named Zack Eswine. There's this really interesting chapter that's entitled, "Searching for Roots." Zack tells this story that he had always lived a busy life and people would always try to get him to slow down. He would work like mad at his job, and his boss would say, "Dude, take a deep breath." He started to pastor at a church, and he would serve and serve and serve and give and give and give just crazy hours. His church leadership team would say, "Hey, Pastor, we want you here for the long term." But he never slowed down until he got a letter in the mail from his mom. And the letter was short and sweet and said this: "Son, if a tree wants to provide shade, it has to have roots."

Moms know best sometimes, don't they? If you want to provide shade, rest, joy, peace. If you want to be a blessing to your children and your friends and your family, do you know what's the best thing you could do? Get to know Jesus. Kids don't need another piano lesson or a soccer practice; they need a mom and dad who are not worried about the future because they know Jesus. Our best friends don't need us to run like crazy doing another thing; they need to know that they're forgiven and that there's joy because Jesus is in control of human history. Just like they tell you on every airline flight, before you try to serve and put masks on other people, put one on yourself and you'll be prepared to serve. Why get into the Bible? Because blessed is the one who trusts in God, and blessed is the one who can be a blessing to others.

Blessed is the one who trusts in God.

That's the *why*. But I promised you a quick *how* too, didn't I? I've learned that whenever I talk about how life-changing and powerful and Jesus-centered the Bible is, sometimes people get fired up. But if you're kind of new to the Bible, you probably have no clue where to start. I remember one guy after a message I preached said, "Pastor, I was really excited to read the Bible. I went to a Christian bookstore, and I stood in front of all the translations. I didn't know which one to get so I went home." Where do you start reading? In the front? In the back? Or should you start with Jesus or the gospels? Let me give you two really quick options to how you could read the Bible if you're excited to start this habit in your life.

The first one is called the YouVersion Bible app; it's incredible. You can download it on your smartphone or tablet and join the hundreds of millions of people who've already downloaded it. It's the most popular Bible app ever invented. On the YouVersion Bible app, you can download Bible reading plans to help you know the life of Jesus. You can do a topical study on anxiety or addiction or marriage or singleness or fear or depression or whatever it is. YouVersion breaks it up into separate days and tells you exactly how much to read. It connects you with Christian friends, and you can dialogue and ask questions. It will push notifications at you if you haven't read it in three days. It knows if you're getting out of the habit. If you're super competitive like I am, it will keep a streak of how many days in a row you've opened the app. It's beautiful and, best of all, it comes at the wonderful price of FREE. It's a treasure trove of great ways to get into the Word. I encourage you to download that today.

My second option is that you work through the Bible in smaller chunks. To read three or four or five chapters in a half hour is difficult. Instead of speeding through the entire Bible, try taking the gospel of John, for example, and reading it in six months. I'm talking about a paragraph of the Bible each day—a few verses at a time. Really take it in and chew on it. Doing it slowly means you can grab it and squeeze it until you get every drop of Jesus out of those words.

To be honest, I don't really care how you do it. I just want you to spend time in God's Word so you can get to know Jesus and can end up blessed. About a year ago, I gave a challenge to my church family: Would you read the entire Bible with me in a year? Eighty-three people said they would join me. But do you know what I realized? Signing up to read the Bible is kind of like signing up for a gym membership on New Year's Day. That's the easy part. There are 365 days of commitment that follow, which is why two weeks ago when I emailed the entire group, I was kind of nervous. I asked them, "How many of you are at least two hundred days into this plan?" I sent the email and a reply came, and then a second, a third, a fourth, a fifth, a tenth, a fifteenth. Forty-five people had been growing in God's Word for the past year.

The best part isn't how often they read the Bible or what part of the Bible they read. The best part was the blessing that

God gave to their reading. I followed up with those 45 people and I said, "Can you tell me the best thing that's happened to you spiritually?"

Here are a few snippets of how Jesus changed people's hearts and lives. Tracy said, "I have learned what true inner peace can feel like." Nate said, "I've been blessed by the time that my wife and I have spent connecting and discussing the Bible together." Julie wrote, "I want to do this every year until the day I meet my Lord and Savior." But Jesse's is my favorite. Jesse said, "I learned that people haven't changed and sin hasn't changed and, best of all, God hasn't and will never change."

God hasn't and will never change.

You know what I heard? Peace. Joy. Love. Fruit. And where'd it come from? A Grow root. Because Jeremiah was right: Blessed is the one like a tree, whose roots are by the water. Even in a season of drought, he or she will never fail to bear fruit. I pray that you and I can become trees just like that.

Your Grow Root

This is what the Lord says: "Cursed is the one who trusts in man, who draws strength from mere flesh and whose heart turns away from the Lord. That person will be like a bush in the wastelands; they will not see prosperity when it comes. They will dwell in the parched places of the desert, in a salt land where no one lives. But blessed is the one who trusts in the Lord, whose confidence is in him. They will be like a tree planted by the water that sends out its roots by the stream. It does not fear when heat comes; its leaves are always green. It has no worries in a year of drought and never fails to bear fruit."

Jeremiah 17:5–8

The cursed ____________ in ______________.

The blessed _________ in _____ _________.

Why grow; why get into the Bible?

Answer: _________________!

Points to Ponder

1. Evaluate: The more you trust your own heart, the less you will need the Bible.

2. Read Psalm 119:1–16, the first verses of an epic song written about the power and beauty of God's Word. As you read, find at least three reasons to grow in the Word each day.

3. Challenge: Download the YouVersion Bible app and explore the hundreds of ways to "Grow" in the upcoming year.

Roots
GATHER
GROUP
GROW
GIVE
GO

Give Generously

In this chapter I want to talk to you about God and money. I know I'm a pastor, and I know you may have had bad experiences with churches asking for money. We've all heard enough stories to realize this doesn't always turn out well.

Before you close this book, I want to tell you three really quick things. Here's the first one: I'm not that kind of pastor. I try to be pretty transparent and confess the things that I struggle with, but I thank God that the love of money and greed and wanting more stuff have never been struggles in my life. I know that's easy for a pastor to say and maybe difficult to believe, so let me tell you a few things that prove it's true.

My car. My next-door neighbor, when

he found out my church was going to put messages on TV, said, "Are you going to get a helicopter?" But my Chrysler Town and Country is my only helicopter. I'm this close to hitting 200,000 miles, and if you cut a $1 million check to our church today, do you know what I would be driving next week? A Chrysler Town and Country. I'm going to drive it into the ground or until Jesus comes back.

I hope in my prayers that God is going to give something to you.

Next, the couch in my house. I got it off Craigslist from Moses way, way back in the day. This couch is old enough to drive my Chrysler Town and Country. My wife despises this couch with its stains and tears. In fact, my family started a fund to buy a new couch a couple Christmases ago, and I spent the money on something else because I'm going to hold onto it until Jesus comes back. You could write a $2 million check today, and I would keep that same couch in my living room.

Finally, my closet. I own about seven shirts. I have one suit—I'm a pastor—I own one suit for weddings, funerals, and all the fancy things in between. And if you wrote a $3 million check to our ministry, I'd be wearing the same shirt next Sunday.

So what I'm about to write about is not about that. It's not about fancy cars; it's not about bigger homes. You could give crazy generously, more than you ever have before, and I would drive the same car, have the same stuff, live in the same neighborhood, and not change my standard of living. This is not about getting something from you. I hope in my prayers that God is going to give something to you; that's the first thing I want to tell you.

The second thing I want to tell you is if you're kind of new to this and you're not convinced that Jesus is the greatest treasure in the world, I don't want you to give anything to a church or to Time of Grace after reading this. If you're not convinced Jesus is worthy of everything. If he's not the sun in your universe that everything orbits around. If you're not convinced he's awesome, amazing, and worthy of every dollar and every cent that you own, I don't want you to give a single dollar or a single cent. Giving is a "get to" and not a "have to." It's something I want to do because I met Jesus and he is so generous and so good that I can't wait to give so that people can hear about his name. So if you have not heard that name just yet or you're not convinced it's worthy to be worshiped, you're totally off the hook. No guilt trips, no fees, no dues, no expectations.

Here's the third thing: If you believe Jesus is worthy to be worshiped, if he's the Jesus you love and trust, do you know what he said about giving? The Lord Jesus himself said, **"It is more blessed to give than to receive"** (Acts 20:35). The Jesus who is God, who knows everything, actually said that what would be even better for you than me giving you $100 is you giving $100 as an offering. He didn't say it's something you have to do or you really should do. He said if you want to be more blessed, don't just try to get; set your heart to give.

That's pretty difficult to believe, isn't it? I mean, when you're a kid, you definitely don't believe this. You can't wait to get the birthday presents. You could care less about your little sister's birthday; you can't wait until it's yours because the presents come. And even as we grow older, it's tough to shake ourselves of that idea. To be honest, that's a big struggle for my church. The other day, I was trying to think about how healthy we were as a church family. We often talk about the five roots that I've been writing about—Gather; are we coming to church group? Are we doing life together? Grow; are we in the Bible? Give; are we generous? And Go; are we inviting people to learn about Jesus? I tried to crunch the numbers as best as I could, and four out of those five roots were off the chart strong. The percentage of people who call our church home, who show up Sunday after Sunday, is ridiculous compared to most churches that I know. This past semester, our Group root is stronger than it's ever been. We had more people sign up to do life together than I think in the history of our church. And we have members who are excited and committed to getting into the Bible day after day.

But then I got to the Give root, and you know what I found? I asked some of our office staff to crunch the numbers to see how many people who are adults and call our church home, how many people gave at least one dollar in the last 30 days? The percentage was 39 percent. These aren't 10-year-olds being counted in the number; these aren't the many guests who come to our church. These are the people who have said this is their church family that they want to support. They've been through the new member process and learn about the importance of generosity. Yet, giving at least one dollar—39 percent.

That number made me think because I feel like our church is in a really good spot. There hasn't been any big drama or controversy. There are things we're working on and flaws and sins we're trying to fix, but there's so much energy and excitement and anticipation about the ministry and yet, in the middle of a season like that, the super majority of people who call it their church home have struggled to give a dollar in a month.

About a month ago, I had this light bulb moment, and I realized why that makes total sense. My light bulb moment was when I was sitting down to write a check to give to our church, and I hesitated. To understand why that was a light bulb moment, I need to explain my financial story. When it comes to people who've lived on this planet, God, I think, has spoiled me rotten with money. I was born in 1980 in the United States of America to an upper middle-class family. By world standards, I'm uber-rich. It wasn't just that my family had means; it was that they were generous and kind. My parents helped pay for my college education, and they bought me a new car my freshman year of college. When I was a freshman, I

I was scared to give.

met a beautiful, talented, godly woman named Kim, who also came from an upper middle-class family. She was born in 1981 in America. And like my parents, her parents were generous and kind. So we met; got married; and, because of our incredible families and the blessing of God, we graduated—all of our education, grad school included—with zero dollars in student debt. Kim and I, our entire adult lives, have never been without jobs. We've never had a single car payment. We've never had a medical bill we couldn't instantly pay. We've never had a credit card that hasn't been paid off by the end of the month. God has blessed us in every financial way that you can imagine, and if by chance something terrible happened and the wheels fell off the bus, we would still have a generous, kind group of family and friends who would take care of us.

But do you know what happened not too long ago? I was scared to give. My quarterly taxes lined up with the tuition payment for our kids going to Christian school and taking piano lessons, and I actually missed two weeks of giving to church. So I was putting three weeks' offerings together, and we had made this commitment to give a certain percentage of our income to the homeless in our community, and I hadn't actually budgeted for that yet, and I was looking at the numbers and hesitated with the pen. I was scared to give.

It hit me—if God has stacked the finances in my favor for my entire life and I can be afraid to give, what's it like when your financial story's been harder? What's it like for you if you don't have two full-time incomes, if you have one or a half or you're searching for work? What's it like if you graduated with thousands of dollars of student loans and then you meet someone who also has thousands of dollars in student loans? What's it like if you're trying to budget for a wedding? What's it like if you're trying to pay for a funeral? What's it like if you're trying to give the lawyers back the crazy amount of money they ask for in the process of your divorce? What's it like if there's uncertainty at your job and you might have an income today but you're not sure tomorrow? I mean, if it scares me to give, what's it like to be others in the church?

Suddenly the 39 percent didn't shock me; it made total sense. You can live in First-World America and you can love Jesus and you can believe he's good and forgiving, and yet when that pen comes out or you open up the app to give financially, something stops you. That something is fear.

So when that light bulb went on, I realized that what I have to share with you is not *how* but *why*. I preach a lot of messages about how to give. You know, here are the options—you can write a check, you can go to the app, you can set up a payment online on our website. Here's what giving looks like. God says you make a plan, you pray about it, you pick a percentage, and you give repeatedly with pleasure because you know Jesus. But I realize all that won't work and won't deal with your fear, unless we tackle the *why* question? Why don't we

Christians need to be afraid to give? Why don't we need to hesitate even though this or this or this or all these things might happen before the check is even cashed?

If we're going to become generous people, if we're going to have a strong Give root that produces the fruit of joy and peace and kindness, we're going to have to answer that question *why*, which is why I love this part of the Bible. About two thousand years ago, the apostle Paul wrote a letter that you can find in the New Testament called 2 Corinthians, and a big chunk of that letter is Paul's encouragement to a group of Christians who felt just like that. The Corinthians apparently had made this commitment that they were going to give a generous offering to help the poor believers in Jerusalem, but between their commitment and actual giving of the gift, they felt fear and hesitation. So when Paul wrote them this letter, he actually spent two entire chapters on financial giving. I want to zero in on three verses, three things that the apostle Paul said. In those three verses you and I will find incredible motivation to become generous people.

Let's jump into 2 Corinthians 9:6: **"Remember this: Whoever sows sparingly will also reap sparingly, and whoever sows generously will also reap generously."** I love the way that starts. Paul says, "Remember." If there's one time that Christians can be forgetful, it's when we're dealing with finances. So Paul says don't forget. Remember there is a God. Remember that God cares about you. Remember that God knows you and knows the future, and he can do anything. Remember. Paul says to remember this particularly: **"Whoever sows sparingly will reap sparingly."** Paul says that Christians should remember what every farmer knows. If you put a couple seeds in the ground, at the end of the season you'll get a little bit of harvest. But if you put lots into the ground, if you sow generously, you'll reap generously in return. Paul is setting up a financial principle for every Christian. He says just like the harvest, giving an offering today won't change you radically. But a season from now, a year from now, a decade from now, if you live a generous and giving life, you will reap an incredible harvest of blessing.

Now let's understand Paul clearly. He's not running a pyramid scheme; this isn't a way to get more money and use God as a tool in the process. Paul's not saying if you give $50 today, by next season it will be $100 in return. Although, you know what happened two days ago? God has a crazy sense of humor. I left my office to run through a sermon on God and money. About a half hour later, I went back into my office, and there was something sticking under my keyboard. I lifted it up, and it was $100. I looked around. Did an angel fly this here? And I went down the hallway to my coworker and I said, "Tom, was anyone in my office?" He said, "Yeah, some random guy just rang the doorbell and gave $100 and said he wanted to give it to the church." God has resources that we don't know anything about. They don't end up in the budget, but God is able to bless us in incredible ways, and God might bless you that way. If you bring him in the middle of your finances, he might bless you financially or he might bless you in better ways. The harvest that you reap might not be more money; it might be better relationships or more trust in God or more joy in spiritual things. Your standard of living might decrease slightly as your standard of giving increases, but God says at the end of a season, you will not regret it. You might already know that.

If you give to a church or ministry, then you're part of sharing the hope ... of God's Word!

I'm actually regretting that I didn't interview a bunch of longtime Christians and ask them, "Do you regret it? You've been giving not just for weeks or months; some of you have been giving for years and some of you for decades. Crunch all the numbers together. How much have you given to Christian ministry in your life? Thousands? Tens of thousands?" Some have given enough money to church to buy a house, and I wish I could have asked if they regret it? I have a feeling they'd say no because those who sow generously have reaped generously. Some are wise enough to know that when you give to support the spread of the gospel, it makes you a part of the harvest of the gospel. You are a part of that! Do you believe it? When you give, you help change a person's eternity. If you give to a church or ministry, then you're a part of sharing the hope and encouragement of God's Word with others! Lives are changed and people are saved and sin is washed away.

I hope you understand that every time you give, it might seem small, but you are reaping generously. The more you see that, the more the cycle of generosity starts to snowball. You give money, and then you hear the stories and you reap generously, which makes you want to sow even more generously. Instead of being a reluctant "have to," giving becomes this incredible "get to."

So what's the first reason Paul provides for giving? His answer is because givers get. We get blessed. We get to be part of something amazing. We get to join God in his mission to save people and to change lives.

God loves a cheerful giver.

But there's more! Paul's not done yet. Second Corinthians 9:6 is amazing, but he's got something else to say in verse 7: **"Each of you should give what you have decided in your heart to give, not reluctantly or under compulsion, for God loves a cheerful giver."** Ever read those words before? This is a top five giving passage in the Bible, and it's so beautiful. Paul says each of you should give, each of you Christians. You might be a new Christian, a longtime Christian, a rich Christian, a poor Christian, a middle-class Christian; each of you, if you love Jesus, should give something. How much should that something be? Paul says you should give what you've decided in your heart to give. I'm not going to tell you an amount or a percentage. Your heart—

which has been changed and saved by Jesus and loves him and trusts him—causes you to sit down, connect, pray, and make a decision. Not reluctantly. Don't hesitate, don't be reluctant, and don't think it's not going to work out. Trust God, and don't let it be under compulsion. My job is not to beat you over the head and tell you to give more. My job is to share the gospel so you want to give, and here's the reason why: Because God loves a cheerful giver.

I love thinking about that. Have you considered your Father's expression when you give an offering? Have you thought about what God is thinking or the expression on his face in those moments? It doesn't say God accepts a cheerful giver; it says God loves—God loves!—a cheerful giver.

That makes me think of a couple months ago. My eight-year-old daughter and I were playing volleyball on a 90-degree day with high humidity. We were in the front driveway hitting the ball back and forth when we heard something from across the street. There was our elderly neighbor reaching up with a broom, trying to get the leaves off of her roof. I could see her struggling; it wasn't going so well. I went across the street and tried to help her out. Before you knew it, we got the ladder out of her garage, and it turned into a big project. This totally train wrecked the special time I had with my daughter. As I got up on the ladder, my daughter ran back across the street to our house, not to pout and be mad, not to hide in the air conditioning from the sweltering heat. She ran into our garage to grab her little broom. And as I pulled the leaves off the roof, she swept them into a little pile. It was hot. I mean, blistering, sweating, uncomfortably hot, and she didn't say a word. We got done, and our neighbor went inside to give us money to thank us. I said, "No, no, no; that's okay." I told my daughter, "She wanted to give us money, but I said no." My daughter said, "Okay, Daddy." We walked across the street, and I was so stinking proud of her. She didn't whine, she didn't complain, she didn't roll her eyes, she didn't get mad, and she didn't regret it. She gave to our neighbor with a cheerful heart, and I loved it. I loved it so much I got out two spoons and a tub of ice cream before Mom could come home and tell us not to spoil our dinner.

That's how God feels when you give, when you see a need and you give, when you don't run away from the opportunity but see someone in your family or in the community in need and you give. You can't see God's expression, but Paul says he's so proud of his kids who give generously and cheerfully and not fearfully. Paul's not kidding. God loves a cheerful giver. What you decide in your heart might be small, or it might be great. It might be all you have to give, and it might be a four-figure check. But God loves it when you think, decide, and give.

Which brings me to the last thing that Paul says. In my opinion, he saves the best for last in verse 8: **"And God is able to bless you abundantly, so that in all things at all times, having all that you need, you**

will abound in every good work." That's so good, isn't it? If you're afraid to give, if you're nervous, if you're skeptical, highlight those words or tattoo them on your arm: God is able. "But, Pastor, what if this happens?" God is able. "Well, what if my debt snowballs?" God is able. "What if this happens with my health? What if I lose my job? What about the stock market?" God is able.

> *At all times, God is able to give you all that you need.*

What is God able to do? How much is he able to bless you? Abundantly. God is able to bless you abundantly. Why give? Because God is able. In fact, he is so able that Paul has this monsoon of big, beautiful words for us, doesn't he? He says, **"So that in all things at all times, having all that you need, you will abound in every good work."** You don't have to be a pastor to sense the repetition, right? At all times, God is able. In divorce times, tax times, braces times, tuition times, uncertain job times, God is able. Up times, down times, rich times, poor times, I-have-no-clue-where-my-next-meal-is-coming-from times. At all times, God is able to give you all that you need. Do you know what you need to live a secure, stable, happy life? God. You need God as the greatest treasure of your heart. He's a big God who loves you, is with you, forgives you, and accepts you. He is merciful and forgiving and took every one of your sins to the cross. That's all you need. If God is your greatest treasure, you don't need a big house or a fancy car to be respected by people who see how much you have. Your heart would be so satisfied in God, and he would be all that you crave. That's why Jesus came. So that whether you're rich or poor, you would have all that you need at all times because God is able to bless you abundantly.

That's Paul's message. Don't be afraid to give, Corinthians. Don't be afraid to give, Christians. God is able, and givers get. What do you think? Are you ready to give? I hope you give in crazy ways. Not so I can get a second suit, but so that people can be saved and meet Jesus. Imagine if we all gave cheerfully because we know that our God is able to provide and bless us abundantly because Jesus was not kidding; it is more blessed to give than to receive.

Don't be afraid of the Give root. God will keep his promise, and it will produce incredible fruit.

Your Give Root

Remember this: Whoever sows sparingly will also reap sparingly, and whoever sows generously will also reap generously. Each of you should give what you have decided in your heart to give, not reluctantly or under compulsion, for God loves a cheerful giver. And God is able to bless you abundantly, so that in all things at all times, having all that you need, you will abound in every good work.

2 Corinthians 9:6–8

Why give? Answer: Givers ______________!

Why give? Answer: God _______ _______!

Points to Ponder

1. Have you ever been a "5P" giver (someone who Plans to rePeatedly give a Percentage as a budgeted Priority with Pleasure because of God's love)? If so, what motivated you to start? If not, what is holding you back?

2. Read 2 Corinthians chapters 8 and 9. List at least five truths about financial giving that you find in these verses (and take special note of 2 Corinthians 8:9 and the power of God's grace!).

3. Challenge: Share your giving plan with a trusted friend, asking for encouragement and frequent reminders that our Father loves to give.

Roots
GATHER GROUP GROW GIVE GO

Go and Tell

The other day I was studying the religious demographics of the county where I live because apparently I don't have much of a social life. I was studying all the different churches over the last 10 or 15 years that had increased in membership and the ones that had decreased. I found some pretty fascinating facts. If you compare the 2000 census to the 2010 census in my county, the overall population had increased by about 10 percent. And yet, most churches hadn't increased by 10 percent. In fact, most churches hadn't stayed even. I found out the Protestant churches in my community, Lutheran churches and Methodist churches, and Presbyterian churches had actually dropped by 5 percent in membership. The Catholic churches had dropped by about 14 percent in membership in that same time period.

But of all the different churches and religions and denominations, it was the last category that demanded my attention. It was a group that had increased by 681 percent. There were only 6,000 of them in the year 2000 but 47,000 by 2010. I have to imagine that number has continued to skyrocket. That group is the "Nones." None. Are you Catholic? Lutheran? Presbyterian? Nondenominational? Evangelical? Protestant? Over 47,000 people in my county would say, "Actually, I'm none of that."

You might understand that number because you're part of it. If I asked you about your spiritual life, you wouldn't self-identify with any church or any Christian denomination or any specific kind of religion. Maybe your parents didn't raise you with a close connection to a church; maybe they did just a couple times a year. Maybe they were every-Sunday people but, you know, stuff happened in life and you started to question the beliefs of your parents. Maybe you ended up without a church, without a religion, without a real passion for spiritual things.

If that's you, this might be a bit awkward; I'm going to write about reaching people just like you, but I hope you find a *why*. Why Christians believe that Jesus Christ is so amazing that if we didn't tell you, if we didn't invite you, we'd be the worst people on planet Earth for keeping the news to ourselves!

If you are a Christian, I hope when you read that number—681 percent, 47,000 people—I hope it messes with your heart just a little bit. Because even if you don't live near me, you can be sure that there are similar numbers all over our country. These are people right near you, people you might meet. These are your people, the people whom you care about and do life with. The people whom you love. These are the people you see when you go out to eat, the people you play bar league softball and volleyball with. These are your brothers and your sisters, your sons and daughters, your roommates, your best friends. They're the good people we love and care about, and so I hope when you read that number, something gets uneasy in your heart.

That's why before Jesus went to heaven, he gave you and me a command. It's something Christians sometimes call the Great Commission or the great mission of Christianity—to go. You go. Don't wait for the pastor; don't wait for some committee from church. You go to the people you know who don't know Jesus and you tell them. You go and let your light shine brightly. Love them, listen to them, no matter what they believe. Invest in their lives. Care about their problems. Pray for them and let them see what it's like when Jesus is at the center of a human heart. Show them that it's how we can find peace and joy and forgiveness despite the craziness of the world, despite the terrible things that we've done. You go and reach people.

That's the hard part, isn't it? *You* go. No matter who you are, no matter how much you know about Jesus, no matter what your personality type, Jesus told each and every one of us to go. All of us should go, and that's pretty complicated. Remember the tree picture with the roots? The Go root is really difficult. It feels impossible sometimes. Have you felt that before? You know someone at work or there's someone in your neighborhood who doesn't go to church and doesn't believe in Jesus. Maybe part of you wants to talk to them about Jesus, but there's something or maybe some things that get in the way. Maybe your personality isn't the type, right? When you go out to Applebee's, you want to eat Applebee's; you're not thinking about the spiritual and eternal future of the woman who's waiting on your table. To start a conversation would be weird and awkward, wouldn't it? Or your kids or grandkids have a sporting event. You watch them and take pictures and enjoy your family. You're not thinking about how you can talk about Jesus with the guy sitting next to you on the bleachers. When you're at work, you're trying to get work done. Intentionally going into every room and every place you are and thinking like an evangelist, like a missionary, that can be awkward. Once you start talking, it can get even more awkward. Talk about sports or the weather and perfect strangers feel comfortable. But talk about the Bible and church and Jesus, and it can get kind of weird. No one wants to be weird. No one wants the Jesus-freak, cram-it-down-your-throat, awkward, where-did-that-come-from kind of conversation. We want to be liked and accepted and loved, and sometimes that doesn't happen when we talk about spiritual things.

Maybe you don't feel qualified. Maybe you have no clue what you would even say if someone asked you to describe your faith. Maybe you feel like your life is too much of a mess to be any kind of example to the people in your world. Maybe the people in your life know that you struggle with addiction or drugs or that you go to AA or to recovery meetings; maybe they've seen your anger problem or they know that you've been through a divorce or two. You're not the perfect example of a Christian life, so who are you to tell them to follow Jesus when you're still figuring it out yourself?

For a dozen different reasons, there are lots and lots of people who don't go. They might give, they might group, and they might gather, but it's been a long time since they invited someone to learn about Jesus or verbally expressed their faith. Now if that's you, if you struggle with that tension, I'm so glad that God decided to put this little paragraph in the Bible. Right after Jesus had risen from the dead and right before he returned to his Father in heaven, he gathered his inner circle together and in three verses answered every question and dealt with every objection that we can imagine. So if you're one of those people who hasn't talked about Jesus with a non-Christian for days or weeks or months or maybe even

If your faith is far from where it should be, you're not disqualified.

years, I want you to pay attention to Jesus' words because they're beautiful and powerful and can change you and help you join this great mission that God has given to all his people. Mark 16:14 says, **"Later Jesus appeared to the Eleven as they were eating; he rebuked them for their lack of faith and their stubborn refusal to believe those who had seen him after he had risen."**

I love that verse so much. For context, you should know in the next verse, verse 15, Jesus is going to say, **"Go and preach the good news."** But what happens in verse 14? Jesus rebukes his apostles. The "Eleven" refers to the 11 guys whom Jesus handpicked. They were in the Jesus Christ School of Theology. They followed him, they heard him, and they saw his miracles. If anyone should have known what they were doing, it was these guys. What does Jesus do? He rebukes them. He calls them out because they were stubborn and imperfect, and they didn't get it. After Jesus had risen from the dead, he appeared to his female followers. They went and told these guys, and the guys stubbornly refused to believe that the women were right. So a verse before he sends them, Jesus calls them out. I love that that's in the Bible. I mean, number one, if you're a skeptic who thinks the Bible is just a man-made book, this is such great proof that it isn't. Some people claim Peter and James and John wanted power and fame and money, and so they handpicked what would make it into the Bible and what wouldn't. But tell me this—if you were Peter and James and John and you were crafting the Bible, why would you let this passage stay in there? "Yeah, you know, after we walked with Jesus for a while, he called us out as stubborn idiots. Yeah, so you should follow me." You would edit that out, and you wouldn't let it make it into the Bible. But here it is, and it's such good news for us. If you're imperfect and if you're flawed and if your faith is far from where it should be, you're not disqualified. In fact, you're the very kind of person who Jesus sent originally on this great mission. Why would a person like you go? Because Jesus sends sinners, stubborn people, flawed people, and broken people. Jesus sends all; your flaws don't disqualify you. The Christian faith isn't based on how strong you are but on how strong Jesus is. Because we follow Jesus, you and I can go.

This makes me think of a dad I knew from my last church. Really solid guy. He went to church a lot, loved his wife, loved his daughter, and loved to worship. But a few years into attending our church, he noticed that his daughter was drifting from the Christian life that Jesus had laid out. He was worried, and he asked me to pray and even speak to his daughter.

I asked him, "Well, have you talked to her yet?"

He said, "Well no, Pastor."

I said, "Why not? You love her. You love God."

He said, "Well, Pastor, when I was her age, I didn't exactly do things right myself, so who am I to speak to her?"

In a sense, I had a lot of respect for that dad. He didn't want to be the overly cram-it-down-your-throat-religious-type parent. He was humble enough to know that he was imperfect and sinful and flawed, but I think at the same time he forgot one thing: Jesus sends sinners. Sometimes, when we mess up, we learn that not doing life Jesus' way tends to backfire. Sometimes after messing up, we learn some wisdom that can help others. More than anything, I think he forgot that when Jesus sends us, he doesn't send us to say how great we are. He sends us to tell how great he is. This isn't self-proclamation; this is Christ exaltation. We don't go into conversations pounding our chests. Instead, we go pointing to the cross. It doesn't matter how messy your life is. It doesn't matter if you're still struggling with addiction. The point of Christianity is not that we Christians are a bunch of really good people who gather every Sunday to become a little bit better. The point of Christianity is that all of us are still pretty messed up, and we need to gather to be reminded that there is still a Savior for broken people like us.

So if we used on Friday night and we had too much to drink on Saturday night and we got in a fight on the way to church with our family, there is still hope and there is still grace because there is a Jesus who is bigger than every single sin.

In fact, I think if you're really messed up, you might be the perfect poster boy or poster girl for the Christian mission, right? If the best person would go and tell her friends about Jesus Christ, they might be intimidated and say, "Well, I'm not that good; I wouldn't belong in a place like that." But if you're jacked up and really messed up and your friends and family know it, well then, maybe they would realize that they too could be forgiven and accepted and included and chosen and saved.

God is sending you because there's a little corner of your community that only you see. I mean, come on, if I show up at your apartment complex or your job and I say, "Attention, everyone! I would like to speak about your faith in Jesus Christ," it would be awkward and weird. Your friends and coworkers would want nothing to do with it because they don't know me. But if you have the same conversation, "Hey, can I talk to you about faith sometime?" That door might be wide open because you've loved those people, and they've come to trust you. You've invested in their lives. You're not some stranger knocking on doors with a handout and a clipboard. You're a person they know and love and trust, and so God is sending you.

He's sending you to say something beautiful; that's what we find out in Mark 16:15. Jesus said to the apostles, **"Go into all the world and preach the gospel to all creation."** That is an ethically important verse for the Christian faith, so let me break it down for you. Jesus starts with this word: "Go." He says, "If you're a Christian, I don't want you to stay. I don't want you to wait. I want you to go." There are people who don't know where to find unconditional love because no one has ever told them clearly, so I hope there's this urgency that keeps you up sometimes at night that you've got to go! You can pray about the guy you work with, that someday God opens a door because you've got to go and tell him. Or how about the guys you play soccer with? You can pray, "Lord, they don't know! They're going to die sometime. They're going to stand before you and maybe no one's ever told them how to stand before you without shame or being condemned. Help me to go."

Where do you go? Well, that's the next part; you go into all the world. You go into the Christian world and the Muslim world and the Hindu world and the Buddhist world and the world of the "I'm not sure" and the world of the "Nones." You go into the straight world and the LGBTQ-plus world. You go into the world of Democrats and Republicans and those who could care less about politics. You go into the world where guys are wearing Make America Great Again hats, and you go into the world of suburban people with hybrid cars and a lot of liberal bumper stickers on the back. You go into that world, into this world, because that's the world that God loves.

Sometimes Christian people make this huge mistake where we assume that "those" people would never, ever come to our church or believe in Jesus. Please take that thought if it's in your head and throw it in the garbage can right now. Does Jesus have a type? The answer is no. He's been surprising people and doing crazy things for all of human history. Who would have thought that God can change the hearts that he's changed, and what's stopping him from changing the heart of the person you're thinking about right now?

Do you know the story about the guy who wrote about half of the New Testament? He was named Paul. Before he became a Christian, he murdered Christians. Do you think at any Christian prayer meeting they said, "Do you know who we would invite to church? Yeah, that guy who's been killing the guys from our church!" No one would have ever thought that that guy would become a Christian, yet he did because God can do the unexpected. So never look at someone in your life and say, "That person would probably say no." The Holy Spirit has a way of making human hearts say yes when they see the beauty, power, and love of God. Jesus is saying go to the people you know; go into all the world.

What do you do in all the world? I love this verb; he says, "Preach." Sometimes people say, "Don't preach at me." They shouldn't say that because preaching is a beautiful thing. The word *preach* in the Greek language means essentially to repeat a message from the king. If there was a king in a castle and I was his messenger and he said, "There's going to be a feast in the kingdom," I would go and preach. That's essentially what Christians are called to do. We don't make up a message; we don't share our story; we preach. We say, "Here is what King Jesus has done and said. Here's what he wants you to know. Maybe you haven't heard him; maybe you've never seen him in the Bible. Maybe you've never read his words, but he has a beautiful message for you. Not my opinion, not my suggestion, but the words of the King himself."

What do you preach? Here's my favorite part: **"Go into all the world and preach the gospel."** The gospel. You know the word *gospel*? It literally means "good news." If you're one of the "Nones," if you're not really a church person, if you had a bad experience with Christian people, I wonder if it's because you were part of a religion that didn't specialize in the gospel. You see, there are two teachings in the Bible—the law and the gospel. They're both good teachings, but church is bad when it only preaches the law and not the gospel. When all you hear are the dos and don'ts, eventually you rebel against it. You realize you can't do all that stuff, and you don't even know why you would do all that stuff. Which is why Jesus says don't just preach the law; preach

There are a million philosophies, there are countless religions, but there's just Jesus.

the gospel too. The gospel is the good news about all the things that Jesus did for you. He knew you would break the law, that I would struggle to love everyone in my life as much as I should, that all of us would try to replace God with something as the first thing in our lives. He knew we would struggle and mess up a million times, and so the gospel is that God himself came down from heaven and every single day of his life Jesus—who is God—lived perfectly and loved everyone. When he died on the cross, he made an incredible trade with you. Everything messed up you've ever done, everything you think God is going to judge you for, Jesus took it all to the cross and died to pay the entire debt.

But he didn't just send you back into God's presence with a blank spiritual bank account. Instead, he gave you and me everything good he ever did. The Bible says it's like Jesus wraps us with this perfect garment, this stainless outfit, so that when we walk into God's presence, we're not stained and flawed and dirty. We're beautiful and perfect, and Jesus rose from the dead to prove that that's true.

If a Christian has never told you that, I'm sorry. If you were raised by Christians and you worked with Christians and played sports with Christians and no one has ever told you that Christianity is about that, it's about the gospel, about a God who loves us when we don't deserve it, a God who did what we couldn't so that we could end up in a place that we wouldn't have without him, I'm sorry. But I'm glad you're reading about it now! And I hope you know this is why Jesus is the greatest thing in the world. There are a million philosophies, there are countless religions, but there's just Jesus. He is unlike any other.

I stopped at a home and garden store and bought some daffodil bulbs. They're these dirty, brown, nasty things that I don't want to touch. Planting these bulbs is going to be messy, and there's going to be dirt under my fingernails. It'll probably take a while. It's going to take a lot of sun and a lot of rain and a lot of work, but what's going to happen in the end? Beautiful flowers. I think a lot of the reason many Christians don't share their faith is because they think about the work and the mess and not the flower. They think about the conversation: "What am I going to say?" "What if I sound stupid?" "What if they don't want to come?" "What if they don't listen?" "What if it takes a long time?" "What if I say something and they don't say anything back and it's awkward for the rest of human history?" We think so much about the process that we forget what could be the end product. We forget what could happen if we preach the gospel and someone we know actually believes it.

That's why Jesus has one more verse for you and me. Mark 16:16: **"Whoever believes and is baptized will be saved, but whoever does not believe will be condemned."** Now Jesus is real; he loves the world, but he says if you don't trust in him, if he's not the center of your universe, you will not be able to stand before God. One day you will die, and God will not compare you to your siblings or your culture. He will compare you to his standard: Did you love Jesus with your whole heart? Did you love every neighbor as yourself? And if you try to do that without Jesus, Jesus himself knows you won't make it. You will be condemned. But it doesn't have to be that way because whoever believes the gospel and is baptized is saved. You will be rescued through simple faith. I love that verb: Whoever *believes*. Right now you can believe that. You don't have to follow 12 steps or have 50 boxes to check. You trust in Jesus. You put your faith in him, and you stand before God. You say, "I couldn't make it without you, Jesus. I'm holding on to your cross," and you will be saved.

That could happen to the person you know who needs to hear about Jesus—your friend, your coworker, your son, your daughter. Can you picture them going to your church? hearing the gospel? believing in Jesus? Can you imagine next Christmas, next Easter, seeing them come? Maybe for the first time as you pray in church, they will close their eyes and start to communicate with God. Can you imagine if five years from now, the people you never, ever thought would join you in your faith started joining you in song at church? The same songs and the same prayers because they love the same Savior Jesus Christ? It can happen. For two thousand years it's been happening because the gospel works and whoever believes and is baptized will be saved.

So why would you go? Why would you take the chance? Why would you share your faith? Because Jesus saves sinners. The people you love, the people who don't seem like they're the type, Jesus can save them. He can rescue them, just like he rescued you.

I'd like to challenge you to think of one or two people who don't yet have Jesus in their lives. Please start by praying for them: "God, please open a door. You love these people, I love these people, but these people don't love and trust in you just yet. Would you please open a door?" I pray that the people whom you thought would never come with you to church would, the people whom you assumed would never believe. That's what the good news does. It changes human hearts.

It did for a man named Alex. Alex and Nate are two good friends who have really incredible roots. They love to gather in Jesus' name. They've been part of life groups and Bible studies. They grow in the Word and read the Bible at home. They give generously and volunteer, and they have gone into the world to spread the gospel with the people they know. But it wasn't always like that.

Years ago, only one of the guys knew God well—Nate. Nate and Alex had become really good friends playing baseball together in college. They became roommates, but only one of them went to church and trusted in Jesus. I asked Nate, "What did you think about back in the day when your roommate, one of your best friends, wasn't a follower of Jesus?" Nate said this: "Alex was always the one I prayed about."

Nate started with prayer, "I just prayed and prayed for my friend." But weeks and months and years went by, and Alex never went to church. Until recently. Here's what Alex says now, "After a dozen of Nate's invitations, I finally agreed to go with him to church. My decision was based partly on my respect for Nate and my desire to attempt to feel what made him feel so content. But mostly, I wanted him to stop asking me to show up. I thought I would go to church, tell him it was wonderful, and then continue with my life. But I showed up once, and I was hooked." That small step kept rolling in an incredible way. I asked Alex what it's like now to know Jesus and to follow him, and he talked about the change in his life, in his marriage, in his faith. He talked about the peace and the joy that he has. And then I asked Nate, "Well, what's it like to see your friend here?" Nate said this: "I can honestly say it is one of the neatest things I have experienced in life. If you had told me ten years ago that Alex would be ushering, joining in groups, banging on the drums in church, and leading at the same church I attend, I would have said you were crazy. It brings me so much joy to know that we share the same faith in Jesus."

That's crazy. But God is pretty good at crazy things, and he can do something crazy in your life too. So, go. Go into all the world and preach the gospel because whoever—yes, whoever—believes and is baptized will be saved.

Your Go Root

Later Jesus appeared to the Eleven as they were eating; he rebuked them for their lack of faith and their stubborn refusal to believe those who had seen him after he had risen. He said to them, "Go into all the world and preach the gospel to all creation. Whoever believes and is baptized will be saved, but whoever does not believe will be condemned."

Mark 16:14–16

Who? Jesus sends ____________________.

Why? Jesus saves ___________________.

Points to Ponder

1. Read Matthew 28:16–20. Find two similarities and two differences with this description of the Go root as compared to Mark chapter 16.

2. Do the same exercise with Luke 24:45–59.

3. Agree/Disagree: If you expect everyone you invite to come to church/believe in Jesus, you will quickly give up on your Go root.

4. Challenge: Write down the names of four people you know who do not go to church. Start to pray for them by name each night before you go to bed.

About the Writer

Pastor Mike Novotny has served God's people in full-time ministry since 2007 in Madison and, most recently, at The CORE in Appleton, Wisconsin. He also serves as the lead speaker for Time of Grace, where he shares the good news about Jesus through television, print, and online platforms. Mike loves seeing people grasp the depth of God's amazing grace and unstoppable mercy. His wife continues to love him (despite plenty of reasons not to), and his two daughters open his eyes to the love of God for every Christian. When not talking about Jesus or dating his wife/girls, Mike loves playing soccer, running, and reading.

About Time of Grace

Time of Grace is for people who want more growth and less struggle in their spiritual walk. We share the truth of God's Word simply and clearly through television, print, and digital media that people view millions of times each month. We connect people to God's grace so they know they are loved and forgiven and can start experiencing a joy-filled life no matter what challenges life brings.

To discover more, please visit timeofgrace.org or call 800.661.3311.

Help share God's message of grace!

Every gift you give helps Time of Grace reach people around the world with the good news of Jesus. Your generosity and prayer support take the gospel of grace to others through our ministry outreach and help them find the restart with Jesus they need.

Give today at timeofgrace.org/give **or by calling** 800.661.3311.

Thank you!